MEDIA ECONOMICS

Media
Economics

*Understanding
Markets,
Industries
and
Concepts*

ALAN B. ALBARRAN

Iowa State University Press / Ames

TO BEVERLY, BETH AND MANDY

ALAN B. ALBARRAN received his BA and MA degrees from Marshall University, Huntington, West Virginia, and his PhD degree from Ohio State University, Columbus. Dr. Albarran is Associate Professor in TV-Radio in the Center for Communication Arts, Southern Methodist University, Dallas, Texas, and Editor-elect of the *Journal of Media Economics.*

♾ Printed on acid-free paper in the United States of America

First edition, 1996

Library of Congress Cataloging-in-Publication Data

Albarran, Alan B.
  Media economics : understanding markets, industries and concepts
  Alan B. Albarran. — 1st ed.
       p.   cm.
  Includes index.
  ISBN 0-8138-2128-2
  1. Mass media—Economic aspects—United States.   I. Title.
P96.E252U616   1996
338.4′730223—dc20   96–513

CONTENTS

PREFACE

Media economics is a relatively new area of study, involving the application of key economic principles to the study of media industries. Today the communications industry is filled almost daily with news of mergers and acquisitions, divestitures, and competition. The impact of technology, government regulation and the growing global economy all has focused attention on the importance of the media not only as information and entertainment resources, but also as economic entities. Students and professors need an understanding of how economics—and economic concepts—impact media companies and industries. By understanding the economic activities of media industries, one can better understand the role, function and purpose of media in society.

Media economics is a relatively young area of research, having gained recognition and stature during the past decade. As a subfield of mass communication scholarship, media economics research is regularly reported in publications such as the *Journal of Media Economics* and other scholarly journals.

Media Economics: Understanding Markets, Industries and Concepts is a book that examines the activities of the mass media from an economic perspective. The book centers on the domestic (U.S.) activities of media companies and industries, and is aimed primarily at undergraduate and graduate students as well as professors and professional practitioners.

Topics discussed in the chapters devoted to specific media industries include the following questions. What is the market? Who are the major players in the market? What is the type of market structure? Is the market concentrated? Are there barriers to entry for new competitors? What types of government regulation (if any) are found in the market? What are the technological forces impacting the market? What is the future for this market?

An understanding of media economics is useful in analyzing the functions and activities of companies involved in the mass media. It is important to recognize that although the mass media serve as agents of culture and vital sources of information and entertainment, the media also operate as businesses with a goal of producing profits. This text examines the mass media as economic institutions operating in a capitalist environment.

Chapter 1 offers the reader a rationale for the study of media economics. This introductory chapter explains the focus of the book and introduces the other chapters and their purposes to the reader. Chapters 2–4 cover principles of media economics. Chapter 2 discusses economic concepts and Chapter 3 centers on understanding media markets. Chapter 4 offers tools and approaches used in analyzing media markets.

Chapters 5–8 cover the broadcast and cable industries. Chapter 5 is devoted to the radio industry and Chapter 6 examines the television industry. Chapter 7 covers cable television and Chapter 8 reviews the economic aspects of the premium cable and pay-per-view industries.

Chapter 9 is devoted to the motion picture industry. Chapter 10 introduces the reader to the economics of the recording industry.

Chapters 11–13 examine the print industries. Chapter 11 covers newspapers and Chapters 12 and 13 review the magazine and book industries, respectively. The future of media economics research is presented in Chapter 14.

Features found in this book include:

- objectives at the beginning of each chapter to guide reading
- review/discussion questions at the end of each chapter
- projects/exercises at the end of each chapter
- a list of references at the end of each chapter
- tables, figures and graphs as warranted
- a glossary of important terms mentioned in the text
- an appendix of materials useful in conducting media economics research

This particular book would not have been possible without my interaction with numerous professors, colleagues and students over the years. Joe Foley and John Dimmick at Ohio State University helped bring out my interests in media economics research while pursuing my doctoral work. Scholars such as Barry Litman, Robert Picard and Mike Wirth stimulated my own interests through their research and writing.

Several reviewers contributed excellent suggestions for improving this text. I have tried my best to incorporate as many of their ideas as possible. In particular, I want to thank Benjamin Bates, University of Tennessee; Robert Bellamy, Duquense University; David Goff, University of Southern Mississippi; and Doug Ferguson, Bowling Green State University, for their suggestions.

At Southern Methodist University (SMU), I am deeply indebted to John Gartley, former Director of the Center for Communication Arts, and Lynn Gartley, Head of the TV-Radio Department, for their unwavering support. Peggy Montgomery and Barbara Scribener were helpful in numerous ways in the main office. Several colleagues, including Darwin Payne, David McHam, Richard DeLaurell, David Sedman and Don Umphrey, read and commented on various chapters. Three different student assistants (Mark Lively, Jeannie Morris and Ione Evans) helped gather research for this book. Lyle Serber assisted with much of the research on the recording industry.

The students enrolled in my courses in media economics at SMU were also helpful in formulating the ideas for this book. Many of the exercises in this book were tried and tested in earlier classes.

The staff at Fondren Library at SMU was of great assistance in compiling research for this book. I want to acknowledge the outstanding contribution of Billie Stovall and staff in the interlibrary loan office, as well as the head of the reference department, Marcella Stark, and her dedicated crew, especially Margaret Bailey. Marilyn Schulte of the Business Information Center in the Cox School of Business at SMU was also helpful in compiling information on research sources.

This particular work is the author's first book, and all beginning authors should have the opportunity of working with a publisher like the Iowa State University Press. In particular, I wish to thank Gretchen Van Houten, Laura Moran and Denise Link for their professional assistance.

Last but not least, my family has been a continuing source of support and motivation in writing this book. My wife, Beverly, who also doubles as my best friend, never complained about the time spent in front of the computer nor my regular stress attacks. My daughters, Beth and Mandy, also thought it was pretty cool that their dad was writing a book. My mother, Jean, encouraged me with countless long-distance phone calls. To them I owe my love and grateful appreciation.

MEDIA ECONOMICS

1

INTRODUCTION: WHY THE STUDY OF MEDIA ECONOMICS?

After reading this chapter you should:

- Be able to distinguish between the terms *economics, media economics, macroeconomics,* and *microeconomics.*

- Recognize the advantages for studying media economics.

- Understand the focus and scope of the text.

What is media economics? Why should we be concerned with the study of media economics? How can an understanding of media economics help in evaluating and analyzing the activities of different media industries? This book attempts to answer these and other questions by examining the mass media as economic institutions.

There are many different ways to analyze the activities of the mass media. For example, there is much interest in understanding the impact of the media on individuals and society. This area of study seeks to find answers to why and how people are affected by media content, and its implications for society. Ratings for television and radio programming help to determine which programs are the most popular among audiences, and box office receipts and rentals of video tapes indicate which movies are the most popular. Critical evaluations of media content enable us to understand the underlying themes behind the programming we see and hear, and the messages they try to convey.

Most importantly, we must recognize that the mass media are economic institutions, engaged in the production and dissemination of content targeted toward consumers (Picard, 1989). Because media firms are economic entities, their behavior is governed by economics. Likewise, consumers are an important part of the economic system. Consumers indicate preference for media content through the exchange of money (as in the case of a magazine subscription or video rental) and time (as in the case of broadcast radio and television). In many media markets, the content is not only designed to attract consumers, but also to attract advertisers who want access to the consumer. Media firms—and the content they produce—are thus influenced by consumers and advertisers. Thus, media content is clearly linked to economics.

The study of media economics provides a context within which one can better understand the behavior of media firms, media markets and consumers (Owers, Carveth, and Alexander, 1993). As both a consumer and student of the mass media, no doubt you have had questions about specific media industries. For example, why did the Fox television network emerge at a time when the other broadcast networks were losing audiences? Why are daily newspapers declining nationally while suburban newspapers are on the rise? Why has there been so much merger activity in different media markets, involving large corporations such as Time Warner, Sony and General Electric? An understanding of the various concepts and principles used in media economics helps to answer these questions.

What is Media Economics?

Economics is defined in many different ways. According to Samuelson and Nordhaus (1992, p. 3), economics is "the study of how societies use scarce resources to produce valuable commodities and distribute them among different groups." Several key concepts in this definition need clarification. *Resources* are defined in economic terms as items used to produce goods and services. Resources consist of both tangible and intangible items. Think of production of a situation comedy for network television—many tangible resources are used in producing the program, including personnel, scripts, cameras, sets, costumes and video tape. The actual time used to produce the program is an example of an intangible resource. Resources are considered scarce because they are finite—the amount of resources available is limited. Further, the individual *wants* and *needs* of consumers, producers and distributors are infinite, further increasing scarcity among resources.

Production is the actual creation of different goods for consumption. In the media industries, different types of production exist; most can be classified into broad categories of print (books, magazines, newspapers), electronic (radio, television, recordings), and photographic (film). Producers make numerous decisions in the production process, ranging from how much of a product to produce to the different types of products targeted toward specific markets.

Consumption is the utilization of goods and resources to satisfy different wants and needs. In the media industries, consumption of entertainment and informational content occurs primarily on the consumer level. As members of the audience, we use the media to satisfy different motivations and preferences. At certain times, we demand news and other informational products; at other times, we use the media to pass time and as a form of relaxation. Another interesting trait of media consumption is that it differs from other types of consumption. After we use a newspaper, television program or magazine, it can be still be used by others. Consumption directly influences the production process, and the behaviors of consumers are an important variable in understanding the economic system.

Using this information, it is possible to define media economics using the Samuelson and Nordhaus definition as a guide. *Media economics* **is the study of how media industries use scarce resources to produce content that is distributed among consumers in a society to satisfy various wants and needs**. In this sense, media economics helps us to understand the economic relationships of media producers to audiences, advertisers and society.

Microeconomics and Macroeconomics

Economists make a distinction between the study of *macroeconomics* and that of *microeconomics* (see Fig. 1-1). Macroeconomics examines the whole economic system, and is primarily studied at a national level. Macroeconomics includes topics such as economic growth indices, political economy (defined as public policies toward the economy), and national production and consumption. Microeconomics centers on the activities of specific components of the economic system, such as individual markets, firms or consumers. Microeconomics examines market structure, conduct and behavior (Varian, 1984).

Macroeconomics deals with:
Political economy
Aggregate production and consumption
Economic growth, employment and inflation

Microeconomics deals with:
Specific markets
Market structure, conduct and behavior
Activites of producers and consumers

FIGURE 1-1. *Differences between macroeconomics and microeconomics.*

It is important to recognize that macroeconomics and microeconomics are interrelated and influence each other. The study of media economics involves both microeconomic and macroeconomic issues. For example, the decision by the Federal Communications Commission to regulate basic cable television rates illustrates the interplay between these fields of study (Johnson, 1994). The decision to require cable operators to lower their rates (a macroeconomic-based decision) affects local cable operators and consumers in specific markets (a microeconomic outcome).

In addition to government policies, technological change can impact the relationship between macroeconomics and microeconomics. For example, the decision to adopt the compact disc (CD) as the primary format for home recordings reflects a macroeconomic decision made by the recording industry. In turn, radio stations and consumers (operating at the microeconomic level) had to decide whether to adapt to the new format by purchasing new hardware and software to accommodate CDs, or to be content with their vinyl record collections.

In later chapters in this text, the study of media economics shifts to specific media industries. As such, most of the material reflects a microeconomic orientation; however, where appropriate, macroeconomic issues will be introduced and examined as well.

The Importance of Studying Media Economics

Having defined and clarified exactly what media economics is, it is perhaps useful to discuss why the study of media economics is important. First, an understanding of media economics is as useful as the study of other "traditional" subjects connected with the mass media. It is just as important to understand the economic activities of individual media markets as it is to understand writing, production, management, advertising and promotion. In fact, one could argue rather strongly that the study of media economics is the most important, in that the ability to attract revenues (and ultimately profits) enables different producers to continue to operate in media markets.

A vivid example of the relationships among producers, advertisers and consumers is in the newspaper industry. Most major cities in the United States are now served by only one newspaper. In markets that have seen one or two competing papers fail, the reasons given are usually the same—the inability to maintain subscribers and advertisers led to their demise. Network television represents another example. The broadcast networks continually introduce new programming to attract audiences and advertisers in order to maintain revenues. If programs fail to attract enough of an audience to cover the network's investment, they eventually will be removed from the schedule in hopes of finding a more profitable replacement. Hence, the economic relationships among content producers and consumers determine much of the media content available for consumption.

Second, the study of media economics is important to your career. If you are reading this text you may be planning—or at least considering a career in some area of the mass media. Virtually all of the media industries are dominated by major companies and corporations (see Fig. 1-2). In fact, if you pursue a career in the mass media, it is likely that you may someday work for one of these corporations. By studying media economics you not only learn how to research and analyze different companies, but also can understand and predict firm and market behaviors. You will be able to determine which companies operate most efficiently, and you can learn which companies are the leaders in their respective markets. This process will not only make you better informed, but also can help you achieve your career goals.

Television:
General Electric, CBS, Fox
Motion pictures:
Disney, Sony, Paramount
Book publishing:
Time Warner, Bertelsmann
Newspaper publishing:
Gannett, Knight-Ridder, Newhouse, Times Mirror
Recording industry:
Sony, Bertelsmann, Philips, Time Warner, EMI

FIGURE 1-2. *Examples of corporations in the mass media.*

Third, a study of media economics will give you the knowledge to analyze different media industries. Through the use of both descriptive and analytical methodologies, you will be introduced to different tools to help analyze the activities of media firms and markets. You will be able to understand how market structure affects the activities of different media companies, how concentrated certain media markets are, and how outside forces such as government regulation and advances in technology may impact future market performance.

The Plan of the Book

Chapter 1 offers the reader a rationale for the study of media economics. This introductory chapter explains the focus of the book and introduces the other chapters and their purposes to the reader. Chapters 2–4 of the book represent a unit called *Principles of Media Economics*. Chapter 2 introduces key economic concepts and their application to the study of media economics. You will be introduced to many different terms and their application to media industries. Chapter 3 focuses on the concepts of market and market structure. You will be able to identify the four types of market structure, and understand how market structure affects the behavior of individual firms. In Chapter 4, tools used in evaluating media markets are presented. Ways to measure concentration and diversification are introduced, along with a discussion of how regulation and technology impact the activities of media markets.

The next nine chapters of the book center on specific media industries. Readers can follow the chapters in their order of presentation, or jump to specific chapters of interest. Each chapter is unique in its presentation of content, and builds on the concepts introduced in Chapters 2–4.

Chapters 5–8 form a unit called the *Broadcast and Cable Industries*. Individual chapters discuss the radio, broadcast television, cable television, and premium cable and pay-per-view industries, respectively. Chapters 9 and 10 are devoted to the *Film and Recording Industries*. Chapter 9 examines the film industry, and Chapter 10 centers on the recording industry. Chapters 11–13 make up a unit called the *Print Industries*. Individual chapters are devoted to the newspaper, magazine and book industries.

Last but not least, Chapter 14 speculates on the future of media economics research. Following the final chapter, students will find a glossary of important terms used in the text (terms found in the glossary are printed in italics throughout the text), and an appendix of resources available to conduct media economics research, including industry and corporate information as well as electronic formats.

What the Book Does Not Do

It is helpful to clarify the limitations of this text. First, this text centers on media economics in the United States, a western country established as a democracy built on capitalism. Although the principles and concepts introduced have broad application, they may not be as useful in the study of media economics in other countries with different economic systems and philosophies. Readers primarily interested in the subject of international media economics should consult other sources.

Second, the mass media are not stagnant industries. As such, change is inevitable, and some of the material in the text will become dated, particularly with respect to data on current industries. At the time of writing, the most current information available to the author was used in each chapter.

Finally, this text is not designed to replace a course in economics. Although the student will be introduced to many key economic concepts, at times the presentation will be cursory. Readers desiring more detailed information, particularly on theoretical aspects of economics, should supplement their learning experiences through other texts and specific courses in the field of economics.

Despite these limitations, it is hoped this text will provide a useful framework for the study of media economics, not only to students and professors of the mass media, but also to industry practitioners and decision makers.

Discussion Questions

1. How does the study of media economics differ from more traditional ways to study the mass media?
2. What is the difference between macroeconomics and microeconomics? Give an example of each.
3. What do we mean by "scarce resources"? Why are resources scarce?
4. What can be learned from a study of media economics? How might the material be useful to you?

Exercises

1. Look through a newspaper for stories that discuss the economic activities (e.g., gross national product, employment statistics, housing starts) of the country. Then look for any articles relating to specific industries such as the mass media, the auto industry or some other industry. How many articles reflect the area of macroeconomics? How many articles reflect microeconomics?
2. Review a recent issue of *The Wall Street Journal*. How many articles did you locate about companies involved in the mass media? Prepare a brief report on one of the articles.
3. Examine the annual index to one of the following scholarly journals and determine how many articles are related to the study of media economics.
   a. *Journal of Broadcasting and Electronic Media*
   b. *Journalism Quarterly*
   c. *Communication Research*
   d. *Journal of Communication*

References

Johnson, L. L. (1994). *Toward Competition in Cable Television.* Cambridge, MA: MIT Press.

Owers, J., Carveth, R., and Alexander, A. (1993). An introduction to media economic theory and practice. In: Alexander, A., Owers, J., and Carveth, R. (eds.). *Media Economics: Theory and Practice.* New York: Lawrence Erlbaum Associates, pp. 3–46.

Picard, R. G. (1989). *Media Economics.* Beverly Hills: Sage.

Samuelson, P. A. and Nordhaus, W. D. (1992). *Economics*, 14th ed. New York: McGraw-Hill.

Varian, H. R. (1984). *Microeconomic Analysis*, 2nd ed. New York: W. W. Norton & Company.

1

Principles
of
Media
Economics

2

ECONOMIC CONCEPTS

In this chapter you will understand:

- How an economic system is organized.

- The differences between command, market and mixed economies.

- The concepts of supply and demand and how they guide the economic system.

- How price affects supply and demand in the media industries.

The economic structure of any society is impacted by the political, legal and social characteristics that influence and shape business practices among firms. The nature of a society's political system determines the environment in which media firms operate. Many types of political systems are possible, ranging from a totalitarian-based authoritarian system emphasizing strict government control to one of laissez-faire, denoting the absence of any sort of regulatory/governmental control.

In the United States, media companies operate primarily in a capitalistic, free enterprise system. Economists refer to this type of system as a mixed capitalist society, with rights primarily in the hands of the citizenry, but where regulatory and other types of constraints impact business practices (Owers, Carveth and Alexander, 1993). In a mixed capitalist society, both public and private institutions produce and distribute products and goods. In the United States, most of the production of media content is handled by private companies (also referred to as the private sector) rather than by government companies and entities (also called the public sector).

Media companies produce and distribute products to consumers in order to generate revenues and ultimately profits in a mixed capitalist society. This system encourages the interaction and interplay among media producers and consumers and, in the case of advertisers, media buyers. Consumers influence media companies by the types of media content they use or demand. In terms of television, local broadcast channels, cable networks and superstations compete for consumer attention (and advertising dollars), along with other forms of video entertainment such as premium cable channels, pay-per-view and videocassette rentals and purchases. Have you ever wondered how all of these entertainment options can effectively coexist with one another?

As for the print industries, there are numerous choices in regards to selecting a book or magazine to purchase. Depending on the subject matter, the options may seem unlimited. There are fewer choices, however, when it comes to reading a daily newspaper. Many cities are now only served by one major newspaper. Why is it that magazines and books have multiplied while local newspapers have suffered a decline?

These questions can be answered in part by understanding the basic concepts of how the economic system is organized. In Chapter 1 you learned that the resources used to produce media content and other goods are considered scarce because there are not enough resources to satisfy all of the needs and wants of consumers. Therefore, allocative decisions must be made regarding how best to utilize existing resources in a society. Economists refer to this decision-making process as the economic problem of a society.

The Economic Problem

The economic problem involves a process of dealing with the important issues of production and consumption. These include the following questions: (1) How much of which goods will be produced? (2) How will the goods be produced? (3) Who will consume the goods? The answers to these questions determine the underlying organization of the economic system.

In addition to determining what goods will be produced, the producers must also consider the quantity of the goods that will be produced and the method of production. Differences exist between the public sector and the private sector in determining the amount of goods to produce. For example, in the public sector, the government makes decisions on how much money to spend for the nation's defense, while at the same time determining how much to allocate for domestic programs such as health care. In the public sector, decisions are often based on social and politically sensitive choices (i.e., social security and other entitlement programs), rather than as a response to specific economic considerations.

In the private sector, production decisions are influenced by the interaction between buyers and sellers or, in the case of the media, content providers and consumers. For example, in the book industry, not only must the selection of which titles to print be considered, but also how many copies of each book to print. Further, publishers must decide the format of the book—whether it will be available as a hardcover, a softcover and/or an audio format. In considering this book for publication, the publisher had to consider a number of different variables including the demand for the book, the likely users of the book and the value of the work.

With respect to determining *who* will produce the goods, individual media outlets determine *how many* people to use in the production of the content. Labor is an important concept in any decisions involving production of goods and services and, in the media industries, labor represents one of the most expensive resources (Dunnett, 1990). In the radio industry, this may involve the decision to use a live, on-air staff or to select an automated, satellite-delivered service. Film directors determine the location for their movies—whether it be in a Hollywood studio or an exotic tropical location; the more elaborate the locale, the more personnel are needed to create the film.

In determining who will consume the goods, certain policies established by the individual media outlets or some form of government may determine who will be able to consume the content. For example, cable television fees vary from city to city and are subject to certain types of regulation, but broadcast signals are available for free. Early in broadcast history, regulators claimed the airwaves were public property, so broadcast radio and television were provided to the public at a very low cost (the cost of buying a receiver and possibly an antenna). Governmental policies led to the establishment of separate classes of broadcast service (AM, FM, VHF, UHF) and, ultimately, created a three-network system that dominated broadcasting for several decades. In answering the three economic questions posed earlier, the government [through the Federal Communications Commission (FCC)] decided (a) how many channels each community would receive; (b) who would be allowed a license to those channels through the licensing process; and (c) that the public would only have to pay for a receiver in order to use or consume the content.

As for cable television, the situation is different. Local municipalities determine how many cable companies will be awarded a franchise (how much will be produced) and also specify the requirements of the system (how the good will be produced). It is left up to individual households to determine whether or not they wish to subscribe to cable (who will consume). When the Congress and the FCC established new cable rate regulations in 1992, regulators sought to encourage greater consumption of cable by requiring operators to lower their fees for basic service.

These two examples illustrate how a society may provide different answers to the three questions that form the economic problem. The type of economic structure in a society influences production, distribution and consumption.

Types of Economies

When a government regulates answers to the economic problems facing a society, a *command economy* exists. In this type of economy, the government makes all decisions regarding production and distribution. The government decides what will be produced and the quantity; it establishes wages and prices and also plans the rate of economic growth. Choice of available consumer goods is limited to what the government produces. Clearly, countries utilizing command economies are on the wane with the collapse of communism in many parts of the world. However, countries such as China and Cuba still represent command economies.

In a *market economy*, a complex system of buyers, sellers, prices, profits and losses determines the answers to questions regarding production and distribution, with no government intervention. The market economy is more or less an idealized economic system and is not truly represented in any major countries in the world today.

In a *mixed economy,* combinations of the market and command economies are found. In the United States, as well as in most of the developed countries of the world, the mass media operate under a mixed economic structure. Typically, these mixed economic systems involve some governmental policies and regulations, while allowing the media to be privately owned. In the United States, the individual media industries establish their own policies in pricing their products, either through advertising or direct payments by consumers (Vogel, 1990).

Perhaps what is most interesting in studying the U.S. mass media as economic institutions is the amount of order that exists due to the elements of the market economy. The observation that the economic system functions in an orderly fashion was first theorized by Adam Smith in a book published in 1776, titled *The Wealth of Nations.* Smith introduced the *invisible hand doctrine,* which suggests that the economy is directed by an unseen force to the benefit of all producers and consumers. Smith advocated the idea of noninterference by the government (laissez-faire) in letting market forces prevail.

Other philosophies recognized that not everyone would benefit from a system of laissez-faire, leading to some segments of society being impoverished and enslaved by the market system. As a result, government involvement led to the creation of mixed economies. Economists have long since argued and refined the concept of the invisible hand as other economic philosophies have emerged, but the idea of unseen order leading the economic system still holds merit. Consider that every day of the year, the mass media is involved with producing and distributing media content, which is in turn consumed in different quantities by various audiences. Yet much more is involved on a daily basis than just production, distribution and consumption.

Take, for example, the daily newspaper. Many scarce resources, such as newsprint, ink, water, electricity and equipment, are used to produce the paper. These raw materials must be obtained from suppliers of these types of products and then converted into the finished product during the production process. Concomitantly, advertisers purchase space in the newspaper in different forms and formats in order to reach the people who read the newspaper. The space must be sold in advance in order to make sure the advertisements meet the objectives of the client. Thus, a system of buying and selling of future advertising space continues on a daily basis. The finished paper reaches consumers in different ways. Some customers purchase subscriptions, though others may only purchase a single paper, such as the Sunday paper, at a supermarket or convenience store. Other consumers may read someone else's paper, and some avoid reading the newspaper altogether.

Supply and Demand

At work driving the market economy (the notion of an invisible force) are a number of buyers and sellers working on behalf of their own self-interests. The newspaper example illustrates in a rather simplistic fashion how the market economy functions, starting with the raw materials needed to print the paper and ending with the creation of the finished product consumed by the consumer. Underlying this example are two fundamental concepts of the market system: *supply* and *demand.* In a market economy, supply and demand mechanisms work together to solve the economic problems of a society (see Fig. 2-1).

Supply is normally thought of as the amount of a product producers will offer at a certain price. Producers determine the quantity, but make most of their production decisions based on the anticipated needs of those who will consume the product. The newspaper publisher purchases enough ink, paper and equipment to produce the daily paper, but will be hesitant to print more copies than consumers normally purchase. In other words, the producer attempts to produce enough of the product to meet the anticipated demand of the consumer. This not only ensures proper allocation of scarce resources, but also enables the publisher to anticipate profits (or losses) based on revenues and expenses.

The available supply of a product is directly affected by the demand for the product placed by consumers. Demand is defined as the measure of the quantity of a particular product or service that consumers will purchase at a given price. The interplay of product, price and market characteristics all influences consumer demand. In general economics, production decisions in competitive markets are based on supply, rather than demand, characteristics. In media economics, demand characteristics are somewhat problematic given the unique nature of media products (content).

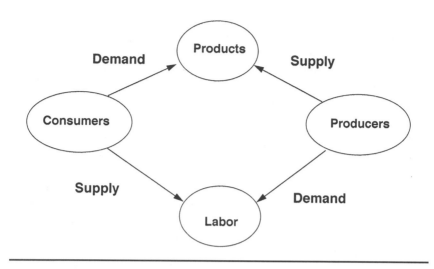

FIGURE 2-1. *The market system.*

The demand curve. Economists use a tool called a demand curve to chart the changes that supply and price cause on consumer demand. Demand curves are normally downward sloping, meaning that as the price for a particular good or service decreases, the quantity (or supply) demanded by consumers increases. On the other hand, if prices are increased, the quantity demanded will decrease. There are occasions in media economics where the demand curves may not follow normal patterns through the range of possible price values; in most cases though, the demand curve is usually thought of as downward sloping.

Figure 2-2 illustrates a typical demand curve. In this example, the demand curve reflects the price of a video recording (such as the movie *A Few Good Men*). Note that the higher the price, the lower the quantity demanded for the product. As the price for the video drops, the quantity demanded for the product increases. When a video distributor prices a new VHS release at $89.95, the product is not really intended for purchase in the consumer market, but instead is targeted to video rental outlets such as Blockbuster Entertainment. Conversely, if the price of the video was set at $19.95, many more consumers would likely consider purchasing the tape for their home library. The demand curve normally holds true for both consumers and markets as a whole, in that market demand is simply an aggregate of a number of individual consumer demand curves.

Elasticity of demand. Change in price resulting in a change in the quantity demanded by consumers is referred to as *elasticity of demand,* or more com-

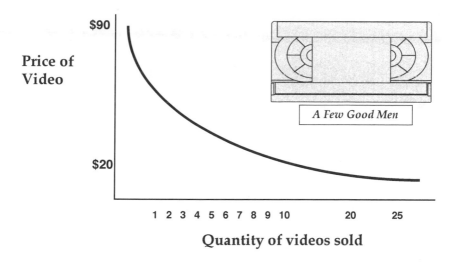

Quantity of videos sold

Figure 2-2.   Demand curve for differently priced products.

monly called *price elasticity of demand.* Economists have identified three types of price elasticity of demand: elastic, unit-elastic and inelastic. The types of price elasticity of demand are presented graphically in Figure 2-3. In elastic demand, a change in price results in a greater change in the quantity demanded. We often see this happen as new technologies are introduced. Initially, prices for certain technologies were highly priced when first introduced to consumers (e.g., hand calculators, VHS VCRs, personal computers), but as prices dropped, many more households adopted the technology. Under unit-elastic demand, a change in the price results in an equivalent change in quantity. Lowering the price does increase the quantity demanded, but on a directly proportionate basis. Inelastic demand occurs when a change in price results in no significant change in the quantity demanded. Lowering the price does not always mean that consumers will demand more of the good; if it is not wanted or needed or has little value, then the quantity demanded will not change. Perhaps this is one reason why eight-track tapes are no longer for sale!

Price elasticity of demand can be calculated by dividing the percentage change in the quantity of a product by the percentage change in price:

$$\text{Price elasticity of demand} = \frac{\text{Percent change in quantity}}{\text{Percent change in price}}$$

A positive or negative sign preceding the statistic indicates the direction of the demand; in most cases, price elasticity of demand is a negative number.

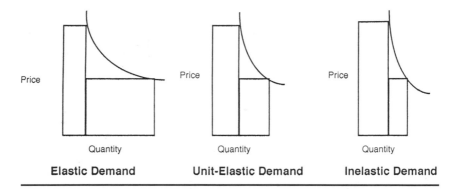

FIGURE 2-3. *Price elasticity of demand.*

Economists use the following criteria to determine elasticity. If the statistic is greater than ±1.0, demand is said to be elastic. If it is less than ±1.0, demand is inelastic, whereas a statistic of ±1.0 represents unit elasticity. Table 2-1 illustrates these price elasticity of demand formulas, how they are defined and their impact on revenues.

Price elasticity of demand is an important concept to grasp in the study of media economics, as it helps to understand how consumer demand is affected by the value of particular products to consumers, and the price at which goods

Table 2-1. Summary of price elasticities of demand

Value of Demand Statistic	Type of Demand	Definition	Impact on Revenues
Greater than one ($E_d > 1$)	Elastic	Percentage change in quantity demanded *greater* than percentage change in price	Revenues *increase* when price decreases.
Equal to one ($E_d = 1$)	Unit-elastic	Percentage change in quantity demanded *equal* to percentage change in price	Revenues *unchanged* when price decreases.
Less than one ($E_d < 1$)	Inelastic	Percentage change in quantity demanded *less* than percentage change in price	Revenues *decrease* when price decreases.

Source: Adapted from Samuelson and Nordhaus (1992).

are made available by producers (suppliers). Price elasticity of demand provides producers with information regarding production and consumption for particular goods, and aids the producer in understanding how demand for products varies at different price levels.

Cross-elasticity of demand. Although price is a very important factor in analyzing consumer demand, it is important to recognize that demand is also affected by the availability of other products (and their respective prices) that can be substituted for one another. Changes in tastes and preferences, demographic characteristics, individual household income and technology all encourage the substitution of different media products or services. In the media industries, a number of competitors produce similar media content, and consumers often sample and substitute other media products regularly. In the study of economics, this process is called *cross-elasticity of demand.*

In a very broad sense, the media industries are engaged in the production and dissemination of information and entertainment content, yet this does not mean that any of the media are interchangeable with one another. For example, to access news, a consumer can use radio, television or the newspaper. Each differs in the amount of time and space devoted to the presentation of the news. They serve more as *complements* to one another, rather than as pure substitutes. On the other hand, a movie on a premium cable channel can usually be accessed in other ways, such as through a video rental store or through direct purchase.

Cross-elasticity is a useful tool in economic analysis, in that it can be used to determine "the extent to which different media compete for different portions of media product and service markets" (Picard, 1989, p. 47). Cross-elasticity has been used in the public policy arena, particularly in analyzing antitrust cases that examine competitive practices in certain markets (Samuelson and Nordhaus, 1992).

In the media industries, cross-elasticity of demand usually increases when there are many potential substitutes, as in industries such as magazines or cable television. In general, studies examining cross-elasticity in the mass media among consumers have shown that as the percentage of income required to consume a good increases, so does cross-elasticity.

TYPES OF DEMAND FOR MEDIA PRODUCTS   It is important to note that there are different types of demand present at different levels of analysis in the mass media. Clearly, there is a demand for the media content by the audiences. Here, demand can be measured on the individual level by consumer usage of the product. This can be studied by examining direct consumer purchases (such as a newspaper, book or movie ticket) or, in the case of content offered for free (such as television), by the *utility* (satisfaction) offered by the product. Typically, utility is a subjective measure, and individuals assign *value* (Figure

2-4) to the content based on the satisfaction derived from the product. Studies of audience uses and gratifications routinely measure the satisfaction, or utilities, desired from media content.

Representative studies by Dimmick (1993) and Albarran and Dimmick (1993) relate the concept of gratifications to economic utility in a series of studies involving the ecological theory of the niche. In calculating measures of utility, the authors found cable television to be superior to broadcast television and other forms of video entertainment in serving audience needs.

There is also demand for access to audiences by advertisers trying to market their products and services to consumers. The advertising industry operates in an interdependent relationship with much of the mass media in our country. Without cooperation, neither industry would flourish. The demand for advertising can thus be studied on an organizational, or macro, level. Most studies of advertising demand have observed little cross-elasticity in the advertising industry. For example, Busterna (1987) found no cross-elasticity of demand for national advertising among several different advertising media, and Picard (1982) found that newspapers are more concerned with industry trends than with with consumer demand in setting advertising prices.

Another type of demand is the demand for media outlets, as evidenced by the large number of mergers and acquisitions that occur annually in the media industries. Most of these studies attempt to determine what variables influence the price of a particular media property—such as a television or radio station, or cable system. In most cases, this type of analysis occurs on the market level, which is the focus of Chapter 3.

What is value? Economists think of value as the worth of a particular product or service. It is a subjective process that is linked to individual satisfaction.

Consumers assign value based on individual wants and needs for a particular product. In terms of media use, this process helps consumers decide what type of media content to utilize in order to meet their needs.

FIGURE 2-4. *Value.*

In addition to the studies mentioned in the preceding paragraphs, a limited number of academic studies have been conducted to determine the demand for media content, advertising and media outlets. Studies are limited because so much of the data needed by researchers are proprietary in nature and are held confidentially by media companies and independent firms. A sample of these studies, the industries examined and their findings regarding demand are shown in Table 2-2.

Table 2-2. Examples of demand studies

Author(s) and Date	Industry Examined	Findings
Lacy (1990)	Newspaper	Competition increases higher quality news operations.
Childers and Krugman (1987)	Cable, VCR, PPV	Significant cross-elasticity of demand observed.
Mayo and Otsuka (1991)	Cable Television	Demand for basic cable ranges from inelastic in rural areas to elastic in urban markets; demand for pay services is also elastic.
Bates (1988)	Broadcast TV Stations	Deregulation had little impact on demand or on price of TV stations.

Source: Adapted from Bates (1988).

Summary

The economic system determines who will produce goods, how goods will be produced and who will consume the goods based on the type of economic structure found in a society. In most developed countries, a mixed economy is in operation regarding the mass media, which establishes a market economy with limited governmental regulation.

The market economy is guided by supply and demand interacting throughout the market to maintain equilibrium. In a market-based economy, supply and demand interact to make the economy function. The mass media are continually engaged in supply and demand in our country, obtaining resources on a daily basis in order to supply consumers with the media content/products they desire.

Demand can be measured at different levels and is affected by many variables including price, value, changing tastes and preferences, and income.

When different forms of media content can be substituted for each other, cross-elasticity of demand exists. Cross-elasticity of demand is a useful tool in economic analysis and is often used in public policy decisions.

This chapter has presented the basic concepts of an economic system and their application to the mass media industries. In Chapter 3, the focus shifts to the individual market level rather than the economic system as a whole. Markets are discussed in terms of their structure, conduct and behavior in an economic system.

Discussion Questions

1. What three questions must a society address in solving the economic problem? How can this be applied to the mass media?
2. What are the differences between the command, market and mixed economies?
3. What is supply and demand? How do they work together to maintain the economic system?
4. What is a demand curve? What are the three types of demand? What do we mean by the terms *elasticity of demand* and *cross-elasticity of demand*?
5. Give examples of demand in the mass media from the standpoint of individual consumers, advertisers and media outlets.

Exercises

1. Investigate the concept of *supply* based on the market in which you now live and prepare a brief report. For example, how many different television stations are there in your market? How many people subscribe to cable television? How many cable channels are available, including premium and pay services? How many video rental outlets exist in the market?
2. Examine the concept of *demand* based on one type of media in the market in which you live and prepare a brief report. Describe the demand for the audience—what do audience ratings and other local indicators tell you about the demand for media from the consumer level? Next, analyze demand for advertisers. Are most channels sold out of their advertising inventory, or does there appear to be a lot of advertising time/space available? Finally, investigate the demand for media outlets in your market—when was the last time a media property was sold? How much was paid for the property? Was it considered a good investment at the time?
3. As a consumer, chart your media activities for a day by keeping track of the following information: (a) type of medium used (i.e., book, radio, newspaper); (b) amount of time used; (c) reason you used the medium (i.e., study for an exam, for entertainment pleasure); (d) other media that could have been substituted for the one you selected (if no substitute available, so indicate); and (e) how satisfied you were from using that particular medium for a specific time period. This summary helps

illustrate how you make decisions regarding media usage, and also illustrates the concepts of supply, demand, cross-elasticity, utility and value.

References

Albarran, A. B. and Dimmick, J. (1993). Measuring utility in the video entertainment industries: An assessment of competitive superiority. *Journal of Media Economics* 6(2):45–51.

Bates, B. J. (1988). The impact of deregulation on television station prices. *Journal of Media Economics* 1:5–22.

Busterna, J. (1987). The cross elasticity of demand for national newspaper advertising. *Journalism Quarterly* 64:346–351.

Childers, T. L. and Krugman, D. M. (1987). The competitive environment of pay per view. *Journal of Broadcasting and Electronic Media* 31:335–342.

Dimmick, J. (1993). Ecology, economics, and gratification utilities. In: Alexander, A., Owers, J., and Carveth, R. (eds.). *Media Economics: Theory and Practice.* New York: Lawrence Erlbaum Associates, pp. 135–156.

Dunnett, P. (1990). *The World Television Industry: An Economic Analysis.* London: Routledge.

Lacy, S. (1990). A model of demand for news: Impact of competition on newspaper content. *Journalism Quarterly* 67:40–48; 128.

Mayo, J. W. and Otsuka, Y. (1991). Demand, pricing, and regulation: Evidence from the cable TV industry. *Rand Journal of Economics* 22(3):396–410.

Owers, J., Carveth, R., and Alexander, A. (1993). An introduction to media economic theory and practice. In: Alexander, A., Owers, J., and Carveth, R. (eds.). *Media Economics: Theory and Practice.* New York: Lawrence Erlbaum Associates, pp. 3–46.

Picard, R. G. (1982). Rate setting and competition in newspaper advertising. *Newspaper Research Journal* 3(April):2–13.

Picard, R. G. (1989). *Media Economics.* Beverly Hills: Sage.

Samuelson, P. A. and Nordhaus, W. D. (1992). *Economics,* 14th ed. New York: McGraw-Hill.

Vogel, H. L. (1990). *Entertainment Industry Economics: A Guide for Financial Analysis,* 2nd ed. Cambridge: Cambridge University Press.

3

UNDERSTANDING THE MARKET

In this chapter you will learn:

- How a market is defined in media economics.

- Different types of market structure found in the mass media.

- How individual firms are affected by market structure.

- How market structure impacts market conduct and market performance.

The market economy introduced in Chapter 2 is actually composed of many individual markets; but what exactly is a market? A *market* is where consumers and sellers interact with one another to determine the price and quantity of the goods produced. A market consists of a number of sellers that provide a similar product or service to the same group of buyers/consumers. Market activity varies across different locations because individual products differ and there are different groups of buyers and sellers. The market for soft drinks is much different than the market for automobile insurance. Likewise, the market for magazines is different from the pharmaceutical market. Yet any market can be analyzed using similar concepts. In this chapter, the focus is on analyzing a market in terms of its structure, behavior and performance.

A market is sometimes referred to as an industry. In reality, a market and industry differ from each other. The market refers to an interrelated group of buyers and sellers, whereas an industry refers only to the sellers in a particular market (such as the film industry) or across several markets (as in the newspaper industry, which is engaged in selling the paper as well as retail and classified advertising).

Today, the majority of media companies participate simultaneously in several different markets. For example, Sony manufactures electronic hardware such as compact disc (CD) players and other audio equipment. Sony also participates in the manufacture and sale of software through ownership of CBS Records and the sale of blank audio and video tape. Sony also owns a film studio, Columbia Pictures, which produces programming (another form of software) for film and television. Hence, Sony is a major "player" in three separate, yet related, media markets. And Sony encounters different competitors, as well as different buyers, in each market.

The Sony example illustrates one of the important aspects of studying media economics: that media firms operate across a range of product and geographic markets. This distinction is clarified later in this chapter in a discussion of product-geographic markets.

Markets Defined: Product and Geographic Dimensions

Picard (1989) explains that media industries are unique in that they function in a dual product market. That is, although media companies produce one product, they participate in two separate good and service markets. In the first market, the good may be in the form of a newspaper, radio or television program, magazine, book or film production. The good is marketed to consumers and performance is evaluated in different ways.

Newspaper and magazine performance is measured through circulation data from subscribers and purchases of individual issues. Radio and television programs use audience ratings, and film performance is measured by ticket sales. Some products require a purchase to be made by the consumer, such as a cable television subscription or video tape rental. Other products may be accessed simply by acquiring a receiver, as in the case of broadcast radio and television. However, all media products require the use of individual time (a scarce resource) in order to be consumed.

The second market in which many media companies are engaged involves the selling of advertising. Advertisers seek access to the audiences using media content. These two areas strongly influence each other (see Fig. 3-1). Greater demand for media content enables companies to charge higher prices for their advertising. Likewise, a drop in audience ratings, reader circulation or other media usage will trigger a decline in advertising revenues.

This dual product market is a unique characteristic for much of the mass media. Most companies that produce consumable products only participate in a single market, that of providing the good to the consumer. Take McDonald's as an example. As a leader in the fast food industry, McDonald's offers a variety of food products to its customers. However, when we consume food from McDonald's, the product is used up. In contrast, media products represent

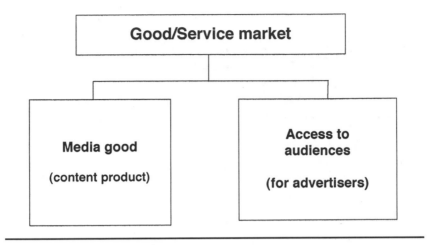

FIGURE 3-1. *The dual product market.*

entertainment and informational goods that can be used over and over again. As such, media firms do not produce typical products, as information goods are not consumable in the purest sense of the term.

In addition to operating in a dual product market, many media companies operate in specific areas, or *geographic regions.* Some firms, such as radio, television, and cable networks, compete on a national basis, whereas other companies, such as local radio and television stations and newspapers, compete in a regional geographic area.

In a few media industries, the geographic region is regulated by some form of government. For example, the Federal Communications Commission (FCC) grants broadcast licenses to specific areas, and local municipalities award franchises to cable system operators. Media industries not subject to governmental regulation simply pick and choose the geographic markets in which to operate.

Defining a media market consists of combining both the product and geographic dimensions (Fig. 3-2). This process delineates a specific market for the media firm in which it offers some or all of its media products to potential buyers. The number of suppliers in a particular market—and the extent of the competition among suppliers for buyers—is affected by the characteristics of the market or what economists refer to as *market structure.* In turn, the type of market structure affects the conduct and performance of the market. A theoretical tool used to understand the relationship of market structure, conduct and performance is the industrial organization model.

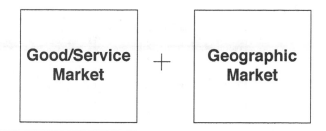

FIGURE 3-2. *Defining the market.*

The Industrial Organization Model

The industrial organization model is commonly used to understand the relationships among market structure, conduct and performance. The industrial organization model (see Fig. 3-3) explicated by Scherer (1980) offers a systematic approach to analyze the many abstract concepts encountered in studying a market. Busterna (1988) adds that the model helps in understanding the interaction of market forces and their impact on market activities. Further, the industrial organization model explains why market performance is linked to market structure and conduct.

In the following sections, the components of the industrial organization model are briefly examined with an explanation of key terms and principles. Readers desiring more detailed treatment should consult Scherer (1980) or Bain (1968), two widely cited sources on industrial organization.

MARKET STRUCTURE   A market is better understood through an examination of its economic characteristics. The structure of a market is dependent on several factors, but several important criteria clarify the type of market structure. These criteria are the concentration of buyers and sellers (producers) in the market, the differentiation among the various products offered, barriers to entry for new competitors, cost structures and vertical integration.

The number of producers or sellers in a given market explains a great deal about the *concentration* in a given market. A market is concentrated if it is dominated by a limited number of large companies. The lower the number of producers, the larger the degree of power each individual firm will wield. For many years, the broadcast networks (ABC, CBS, NBC) dominated the network television market, particularly with respect to advertising. But as cable television, other video technologies and the Fox Broadcasting Company emerged as competitors, competition for viewers and advertisers intensified.

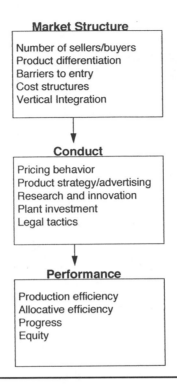

FIGURE 3-3. *Industrial organization model.* (Modified from Scherer, 1980)

Concentration can be measured in different ways, but in media economics two approaches prevail. One method measures the percentage of the market (using circulation or ratings data) reached by competitors through the product. Another method involves calculating the percentage of revenues (sales) controlled by the top four (or eight) firms. These ratios are discussed more fully in Chapter 4.

Product differentiation refers to the subtle differences (either real or imagined) perceived by buyers to exist among products produced by sellers. A number of magazines are geared to specific markets. For example, there are several publications targeted toward the world of business. Yet *Forbes, Business Week,* and *Money* all present different editors, columnists and other features geared toward their readers. Radio stations offer a variety of music formats, and their call letters, personalities, marketing campaigns and technical facilities create differences from one station to the next.

Barriers to entry are normally thought of as obstacles new sellers must overcome before entering a particular market. Barriers may be limited to capital (money) or other factors. Wirth (1986) studied barriers to entry for the newspaper and broadcast industries and found that entry into the newspaper business involved far more economic barriers than did entry into broadcast radio or television. Before Rupert Murdoch could purchase a set of television stations in order to establish the Fox network, he first had to meet a number of federally mandated ownership criteria (including obtaining U.S. citizenship) in order to be approved by the FCC.

Cost structures consider the costs for production in a particular market. Total costs consist of both fixed costs—the costs needed to produce one unit of a product—and variable costs—costs that are variable in nature depending on the quantity produced (e.g., labor and raw materials). Industries that have high fixed costs, such as newspapers and cable television, often lead to highly concentrated markets. *Economies of scale* usually exist in these situations for the producer (seller). By economies of scale, we refer to the decline in average cost that occurs as additional units of a product are created.

Vertical integration occurs when a firm controls different aspects of production, distribution and exhibition of its products (Fig. 3-4). Time Warner Entertainment is an example of a company engaged in vertical integration. A movie produced by the Time Warner–owned Warner Brothers film studio eventually will appear on pay-per-view on Time Warner cable systems. Following pay-per-view, the movie will likely be scheduled on premium services such as Home Box Office or Cinemax. Finally, the movie may be offered as a package of feature films for sale to cable networks or local television stations. Time Warner maximizes its revenue for the film through the different stages of distribution and exhibition.

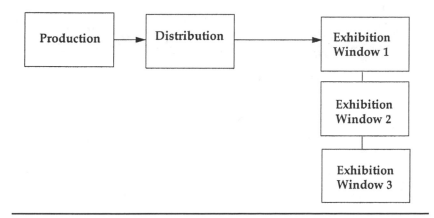

FIGURE 3-4. *Vertical integration.*

Analyzing the number of producers and sellers in a market, the difference between products, barriers to entry, cost structures and vertical integration gives insight into the structure of a market. Four types of market structure serve as theoretical models. These four types of market structure are recognized popularly in much of the literature as the "theory of the firm" (Litman, 1988).

The theory of the firm. The four types of market structure are monopoly, oligopoly, monopolistic competition and perfect competition. The four market structures represent a continuum, with monopoly and perfect competition found at opposite ends, and oligopoly and monopolistic competition occupying interior positions (Fig. 3-5). These types of market structure are represented in different industries, including the mass media.

A *monopoly* is a type of structure whereby a single seller of a product exists and thus dominates the market. Generally, a monopolistic structure assumes there is no clear substitute for the product; a buyer must purchase the good from the monopolist or avoid consumption of the good altogether. Because of this, economists refer to monopolists as "price-makers," as they can set the price in order to maximize profits. As expected, barriers to entry are very high in a monopoly.

The monopolist can also exhibit power in the market by restricting production output (if desired). In a monopolistic structure, the demand curve for the product is the same as the industry demand curve (Fig. 3-6). If no close substitute exists, demand is generally perceived as inelastic. It is important to recognize that not all consumers (buyers) demand the seller's product. If demand is weak and substitutes emerge, the monopolist will have little market power.

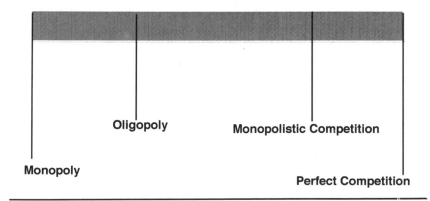

FIGURE 3-5. *Market structure.*

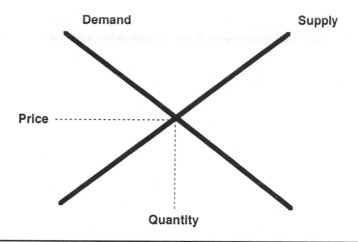

FIGURE 3-6. *Monopoly demand curve.*

An *oligopoly* differs from a monopoly in that an oligopolistic structure features more than one seller of a product. Products offered by the sellers may be either homogeneous or differentiated. Typically, a market dominated by a few firms is considered an oligopoly, and each firm commands a similar share. Firms in an oligopoly are mutually interdependent, with the actions of the leading firm(s) affecting the other firms in the market. These firms consider their actions in light of the impact on the market and their competitors. Depending on the reaction of other competitors, changes made by the leader(s) may move firms in an oligopoly toward more cooperation or competition.

In an oligopoly, price is normally set by the leader, and others follow suit. The small number of sellers and the lack of substitutes create an inelastic demand curve for the oligopolistic market structure (see Fig. 3-7). Barriers to entry may take several forms in an oligopoly, but they are not as significant as those found in a monopoly. For example, the Fox network was able to enter the television network market successfully despite the fact that ABC, CBS and NBC held dominance with audiences, advertisers and affiliates.

A third type of market structure, *monopolistic competition,* exists when there are many sellers offering products that are similar, but not perfect, substitutes for one another. Barriers to entry are lower than those found in an oligopoly. Each firm attempts to differentiate its products in the minds of the consumer through various methods including advertising, promotion, location, service and quality.

Unlike in the oligopoly, price varies in this type of market structure with

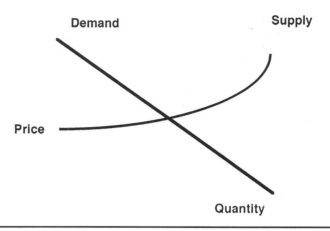

FIGURE 3-7. *Monopolistic competition demand curve.*

price decisions set by both the market and the individual firms. Monopolistic competitive firms, believing they operate independently in the market, will often lower prices in order to increase revenue. However, other competitors facing similar conditions may also lower their prices, which results in a downward-sloping demand curve (see Fig. 3-8) for the market.

In *perfect competition,* the market structure is characterized by many sellers in which the product is homogeneous and no single firm or group of firms dominates the market. With no barriers to entry, the characteristics of the market economy dominate in a perfectly competitive market structure.

Individual firms operate as "price-takers," in that the market sets the price for the product, and prices are naturally constrained downward (Picard, 1989). The only production decision the firm makes in this type of market structure is how much of the good to produce, as it has no control over price. The demand and supply curves are straight under perfect competition (see Fig. 3-9).

MEDIA INDUSTRIES AND MARKET STRUCTURE   In order to apply the theory of the firm to the media industries, one must first understand the specific market and the number of firms operating in the market and determine the amount of control the firm(s) has over its competitors. Media industries occupy different positions across the four types of market structure shown in Figure 3-10.

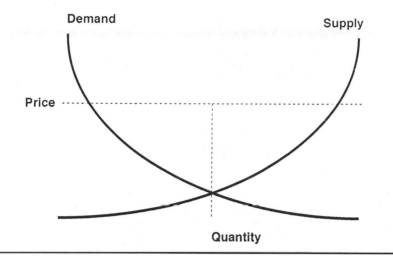

FIGURE 3-8. *Oligopoly demand curve.*

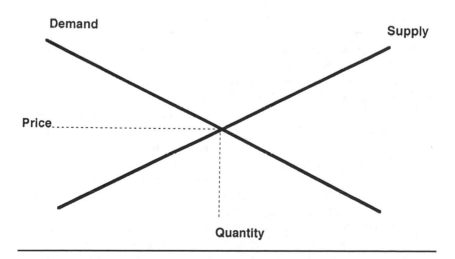

FIGURE 3-9. *Demand curves in perfect competition.*

- **Monopoly**
  - Cable television
  - Newspapers (in most markets)
- **Oligopoly**
  - Television networks
  - Motion pictures
  - Recording industry
- **Monopolistic competition**
  - Books
  - Magazines
  - Radio

FIGURE 3-10. *Key media industries by market structure.*

The closest example of a monopoly market structure in the mass media is cable television. Cable systems are locally regulated according to franchise agreements established between the cable operator and the local form of government and are specified for a set period of time. The cable industries' monopoly position is being threatened by competition from local telephone companies and direct-broadcast satellite systems, as well as other competitors.

Newspapers tend to fall in either a monopolistic or oligopolistic structure depending on the number of newspapers published in a particular geographic area. The number of cities served by more than one daily newspaper has declined rapidly over the past few decades (see Fig. 3-11), suggesting a move toward a monopolistic structure.

For the most part, broadcast television stations operate in an oligopolistic market structure, as do the broadcast networks. The TV industry utilizes the same types of programming—situation comedies, dramas, movies, sports, news, reality, etc. The product is relatively homogeneous, although competition for audiences is intense. Other industries with an oligopolistic structure include the motion picture and recording industries.

A number of media industries fall under the monopolistic competition market structure, including the magazine, book and radio industries. Although each of these industries differs in terms of barriers to entry and product differentiation, they are all best described as monopolistic competitive. A true perfectly competitive market structure does not exist in the mass media.

Scherer's two-dimensional model. The theory of the firm helps clarify the distinctions found across the four types of market structure. In addition to the

Year	Number of Cities
1954	88
1959	81
1965	70
1975	65
1980	57
1990	43
1994	33

FIGURE 3-11. *Cities with two or more newspapers.* (Newspaper Association of America, 1994)

theory of the firm, Scherer (1980) offers a two-dimensional approach to understanding market structure (Fig. 3-12). The first dimension considers the number of sellers in a market (one, a few, many) and the second dimension separates homogeneous products from differentiated products.

This two-dimensional approach is helpful in clarifying some aspects of market structure left unanswered by the theory of the firm. This is evident in Scherer's distinction between homogeneous oligopolies and differentiated oligopolies. An example of a homogeneous oligopoly would be the broadcast TV networks and their relationships with advertisers. In this sense, the networks are similar; from an advertiser's view they each offer access to audiences in the same way. An example of a differentiated oligopoly would be the case of a city served by more than one newspaper. *The New York Times* is a different product than the *New York Post,* just as the *Chicago Tribune* is a different paper from the *Sun-Times.*

Both the theory of the firm and Scherer's seller/product dimensions are helpful in understanding market structure. The following sections focus on how market structure influences market conduct and market performance, the other components of the industrial organizational paradigm.

MARKET CONDUCT   *Market conduct* refers to the policies and behaviors ex-
hibited by sellers and buyers in a market. Market conduct centers around five specific areas: pricing behavior, product strategy and advertising, research and innovation, plant investment, and legal tactics. Of special interest is how

Type of Product	Number of Firms		
	One	A Few	Many
Homogeneous product	Pure monopoly	Homogeneous oligopoly	Pure competition
Differentiated product	Pure monopoly	Differentiated oligopoly	Monopolistic competition

FIGURE 3-12. *Scherer's two dimensions of market structure.* (Scherer, 1980)

these different types of behaviors appear to be coordinated among firms in certain types of market structure.

Pricing policies or behaviors are the most observable type of market conduct. Here, the interest is understanding how pricing policies are established. Picard (1989) explains that pricing policies involve a series of decisions regarding how products are packaged, discounted and set. Picard identifies four common price orientations: (a) demand-oriented pricing, where prices are set via market forces; (b) target return pricing, which is based on a desired amount of profit; (c) competition oriented pricing, in which prices are based on those offered by competitors; and (d) industry norm pricing, which is based on the industry at large, rather than market forces.

Product strategy and advertising refer to decisions based on the actual products offered by a firm, including how a product is packaged or designed. In the media industries, it may involve what type of programming to secure for a new cable channel, the type of music format selected for an FM radio station, or the quality of paper on which to print a magazine. As discussed previously, firms must also consider which market to enter from a geographic perspective, by targeting a national audience or concentrating on specific areas.

Advertising entails a range of activities designed to create awareness of media products and services. Promotional and marketing activities aimed at consumers are ultimately designed to increase market share at the expense of other competitors. Clearly, in more competitive types of market structure, advertising is vital in order for media products to maintain an image and position in a market.

Research and innovation refer to the effort of firms to differentiate or improve their products over time. Because of the insatiable appetite that consumers have for media content, continuing emphasis is placed on research in order to better understand the behaviors and characteristics of media consumers. Further, technological innovations have enabled media content to be delivered to consumers faster, more accurately and with more options. This forces other firms to respond in order to remain competitive in their individual markets.

Plant investment refers to the different resources needed to create or purchase the physical plant in which goods will be produced. Some of the mass media industries involve a significant investment in capital and physical plant. In particular, newspapers, motion pictures and cable television require a sizeable investment on the part of participants.

Legal tactics encompass the entire range of legal actions utilized by a firm in a particular market. The most visible use of legal tactics occurs through the use of patents and copyrights for particular goods. The history of the electronic media in the United States is replete with examples of patent disputes, particularly in the development of the radio industry. Copyright is still very important today, as video and audio piracy (illegal copying and distribution of copyrighted material) creates millions of dollars of lost revenue for the film and recording industries (Vivian, 1995).

MARKET PERFORMANCE   *Market performance* involves analyzing the ability of individual firms in a market to achieve goals based on different performance criteria. Market performance is usually evaluated from a societal perspective, rather than from the level of the firm. Policy makers can examine the economic efficiency of a particular industry through performance criteria and, if necessary, initiate structural or market conduct solutions to remedy problems. In this sense, performance is examined from a macroeconomic orientation. A number of variables including efficiency, equity and progress are considered in evaluating market performance.

Efficiency refers to the ability of a firm to maximize its wealth. Normally, two types of efficiency are reviewed: technical efficiency and allocative efficiency. *Technical efficiency* involves using the firm's resources in the most effective way to maximize output. Much of the conglomeration that has occurred in the media industries is designed to increase technical efficiency through mergers and acquisitions, which create economies of scale. *Allocative efficiency* occurs when an individual market functions at an optimal capacity, spreading its benefits among producers and consumers. Conversely, excess profits are often seen as allocative inefficiency, as they suggest that market resources are being used improperly. Normally, the solution is to encourage more competitors in the market in order to lower profits to more optimal levels. Decisions to limit ownership for television and radio stations encourage allocative efficiency as well as diversity of expression.

Equity is concerned with the way in which wealth is distributed among producers and consumers. Ideally, a market economy system will provide a fair distribution of equity so that no single firm receives excessive rewards. Naturally, equity is more problematic in monopolistic and oligopolistic market structures, where wealth is more concentrated among firms.

Progress refers to the ability of firms in a market to increase output over time. Progress goals are set by each firm, and evaluations for the market are determined by the aggregate sum of market output. Statistical data are compiled by various trade associations and some governmental agencies to monitor progress in different markets.

As the industrial organizational model implies, the structure of the market affects the conduct of different firms in a market, which in turn impacts the performance of the market. This framework is valuable in the study of media economics because it provides both theoretical and practical utility in the analysis of different types of media industries, as well as providing substance to abstract concepts.

Summary

This chapter has focused on understanding an individual market in media economics by introducing one of the unique aspects of media economics: the dual dimensions of product and geography used in defining a market. The industrial organization model is used to recognize how market structure, market conduct and market performance are linked together.

Market structure can be identified using several different criteria, including the concentration of buyers and sellers in the market, the differentiation among products, the barriers to entry for new competitors, cost structures and vertical integration. Media industries operate along a continuum involving four models of market structure: monopoly, oligopoly, monopolistic competition and perfect competition.

Market structure affects the market conduct of individual firms and is concerned with pricing behaviors, product strategy and advertising, research and innovation, plant investment and legal tactics. The conduct of firms in a market likewise impacts the performance of the market. Market performance is evaluated most often from a macro perspective with respect to different performance variables including efficiency, equity and progress.

In Chapter 4, emphasis is placed on evaluating individual media markets. Methods used to compare different markets are discussed and tools for analysis are introduced, along with a discussion on how regulation and technology may affect market behavior.

Discussion Questions

1. What does it mean to say the mass media operate in a dual product market? Give examples based on your local media.
2. What are the basic differences between the four types of market structure introduced in the chapter?
3. Identify the following terms in regards to analyzing a media market: *product differentiation, barriers to entry,* and *concentration.*
4. What is the difference between market conduct and market performance? How does market structure influence market conduct? How does market structure influence market performance?

Exercises

1. Examine the local media in your market, and categorize them in terms of the four types of market structure discussed in the chapter. Is there any type of structure not represented in your market? Are there any indications that one of the media markets may be moving toward a different type of structure? Explain.
2. Compare the news operations among the local television, radio and newspaper outlets. Each outlet is engaged in the distribution of news, but it presents its product differently. How do they differ?
3. You are a media consultant in your local market. A group of investors desire your services as they are interested in starting a new media outlet in your market. Determine the barriers to entry that exist for starting the following types of new media facilities in your local market: (a) daily newspaper; (b) an FM radio station; (c) a UHF television station; and (d) a new cable system. What would you advise your clients to do?

References

Bain, J. S. (1968). *Industrial Organization.* New York: John Wiley & Sons.

Busterna, J. C. (1988). Concentration and the industrial organizational model. In: Picard, R.G., McCombs, M., Winter, J. P., and Lacy S. (eds.). *Press Concentration and Monopoly: New Perspectives on Newspaper Ownership and Operation.* Norwood, NJ: Ablex Publishing Company, pp. 35–53.

Compaine, B. M. (1985). *Who Owns the Media?,* 2nd ed. White Plains, NY: Knowledge Industry Publications.

Litman, B. R. (1988). Microeconomic foundations. In: Picard, R.G., McCombs, M., Winter, J. P., and Lacy S. (eds.). *Press Concentration and Monopoly: New Perspectives on Newspaper Ownership and Operation.* Norwood, NJ: Ablex Publishing Company, pp. 3–34.

Newspaper Association of America (1994). *Facts About Newspapers.* Reston, VA:

Newspaper Association of America.

Picard, R. G. (1989). *Media Economics.* Beverly Hills: Sage.

Scherer, F. M. (1980). *Industrial Market Structure and Economic Performance,* 2nd ed. Chicago: Rand McNally. (Figures 3-3 and 3-12 also appear in Scherer, F. M. and Ross, D. 1990. *Industrial Market Structure and Economic Performance,* 3rd. ed. Boston: Houghton Mifflin. Reprinted with permission.)

Varian, H. R. (1984). *Microeconomic Analysis,* 2nd ed. New York: W. W. Norton & Company.

Vivian, J. (1995). *The Media of Mass Communication,* 3rd ed. Needham Heights, MA: Allyn & Bacon.

Wirth, M. O. (1986). Economic barriers to entering media industries in the United States. In: McLaughlin, M. (ed.). *Communication Yearbook,* 9. Beverly Hills, CA: Saje, pp. 423–442.

4

EVALUATING MEDIA MARKETS

In this chapter you will learn:

- Where to locate resources for information on media industries and individual firms.

- Methods used to measure market concentration.

- How to measure diversification within a firm.

- How regulation affects media markets and individual firms.

- How technology affects media markets and individual firms.

n understanding of market structure, conduct and performance is vital in order to analyze media markets properly. Theoretical models of market structure, such as oligopoly and monopolistic competition, provide descriptive information that clarifies the nature and extent of supply, demand, competition and barriers to entry.

Although this information is useful, it is helpful to have more precise analytical information with which to evaluate media markets carefully. In this chapter, you will be introduced to a variety of resources and methodologies to enable you to evaluate media firms and markets.

There are several reasons why an evaluation of media markets is important. First and perhaps most important to this text, an evaluation of media markets enables you to understand the various processes at work that cause media companies to operate in the manner in which they do. Every month seems to bring news of yet another proposed merger, acquisition or divestiture involving media companies. By understanding the economic characteristics of individual firms and markets, and by having the tools with which to analyze their activities, one can better comprehend the role and function of the media in society.

Second, evaluating media markets is important for group and individual investment purposes. A majority of the companies engaged in the mass media are *public companies,* meaning they are publicly owned by individual and institutional stockholders who invest in a firm in hopes of obtaining profits through stock appreciation and corporate dividends. Brokerage firms and other analysts constantly monitor media market performance in order to pass along recommendations to buy, sell or hold shares in publicly traded companies. Prudent investing is thus contingent on the use of accurate information in making these important decisions.

Third, if you are considering employment in some aspect of the mass media, it is essential that you understand the economic characteristics of the individual market in which you wish to work. This will help you to identify the potential employers, understand the lines of business in which they are engaged and determine their position in the market—all factors that can impact your potential for salary, advancement and job stability. Surprisingly, many college graduates send resumes to potential employers without any understanding or investigation of the individual company, its ownership or financial condition.

In the following sections of the chapter, you are introduced to different resources used in evaluating media markets. Many of these resources are available in public and university libraries, as well as from individual companies. Later, methodological tools are introduced to provide measurements of market concentration. Finally, a discussion of exterior forces in the form of regulation and technology completes this examination of evaluating media markets.

What Is the Media Market?

In Chapter 3, we learned that a market is where consumers and sellers interact with one another to determine the price and quantity of the goods produced. Further, in defining a market, one must consider the geographic boundaries in which the market is engaged. However, defining media markets can be a difficult process. As Bates (1993, p. 4) has observed, "media markets are no longer neatly defined" due to increasing competition, close substitutes and geographic boundaries, which overlap on several levels.

For example, consider two markets in which the radio industry is engaged. Nationally, there are approximately twenty-five radio networks, which form a market that serves national advertisers and individual radio stations. National advertisers, working primarily through advertising agencies in media planning, use radio networks to help target specific audiences. Local radio stations may affiliate with a radio network to obtain specific news and features delivered by the network to supplement their local format.

On the local level, there are over ten thousand radio stations operating in the United States. But the majority of these stations tend to be clustered in different geographic locations (or "markets," as the radio industry uses the term). In Top-10 markets, as many as 40 to 50 different radio stations may be scattered among the AM/FM band, with a variety of different formats. Clearly, not all stations compete for the same listeners and advertisers in the local economy, as different formats attract different groups of buyers and sellers.

Precise definitions of media markets are problematic without specific criteria. In defining a media market, researchers normally consider specific geographic boundaries, such as the international, national, regional or local market. Next, consideration is given to distinct areas, such as the market for advertisers or the market for audiences, both of which serve as indications of demand. Other areas can be used in defining the market, such as the number of sellers (suppliers) or the share of the market (e.g., advertising revenue, audience ratings or circulation data) held by each firm. Clearly, defining a market is not a cursory task, but a process involving careful analysis and decision making.

Who Are the Major Players in the Market?

Once the market is defined, attention can be turned to learning who are the major companies or "players" in the market or industry. There are many different resources to consult to obtain this information, and Appendix A to this text lists a number of resources normally available at most libraries. The following headings list some of the most useful sources.

Industry Sources. Libraries contain numerous directories and reference volumes for many individual industries. *The Standard Industrial Classification (SIC) Manual* provides a complete listing of different industries using the SIC code, and is a good starting point if you know little about a particular industry. It categorizes the U.S. economy by numbered segments or codes.

Researchers and analysts use the SIC codes in tabulating economic and financial data for the economy. The SIC system covers economic activity in nine major categories: agriculture, forestry and fishing; mining; construction; manufacturing; transportation, communications and public utilities; wholesale trade; retail trade; finance, insurance and real estate; and services. These categories are further divided into major groups, identified by two-digit codes; then into industry groups, with three-digit codes; and, finally, into industries, using four-digit codes.

Industries are arranged in alphabetical order and each industry has a unique numeric code. For example, all companies involved in broadcast television are assigned a code of 4833, cable television services, 4841, and newspaper publishers, 2711. Once you know the SIC code for a particular industry, you can use the code to identify individual companies engaged in that industry. Several different directories show SIC code listings.

Standard & Poor's Industry Surveys, published since 1973, provides analyses of different industries and comparative financial statistics for key companies in each featured industry. The listing of companies in each industry is not exhaustive, but it does offer a quick review of the major players. The material is published quarterly.

Another useful source is the *U.S. Industrial Outlook,* a government publication. This source provides an overview of recent trends and financial outlook for some two hundred industries, including many different media-related industries. This annual publication, which began in 1960, was discontinued with the 1994 edition.

One other source for industry data is the *Value Line Investment Survey.* This particular resource provides reports on over 75 different industry groups and also analyzes some 1,500 companies. The Value Line service is used heavily by brokerage analysts and individual investors seeking more information on a particular company or industry.

Finally, industry-specific directories such as the *Broadcasting/Cablecasting Yearbook,* the *Television and Cable Factbook,* and the *Editor and Publisher International Yearbook* should be consulted as well. These directories are usually annual publications and contain some economic data.

Company directories. A number of directories are useful to obtain more information on specific corporations. Dun & Bradstreet, Inc. publishes a number of different directories including the *Million Dollar Directory*, *America's Corporate Families, America's Corporate Families and International Affiliates*, and *Dun & Bradstreet's Business Rankings.* Each of these publications differs in terms of their specific coverage of different companies, but most contain standard information such as SIC code indexes, parent/subsidiary cross references, company profiles, employment statistics and annual sales/revenues.

Additionally, *Ward's Business Directory of U.S. Private and Public Companies* is a very useful source to locate information on *private companies*—those not owned by the public and thus not available on any stock market. *Standard & Poor's Register of Corporations, Directors and Executives* is an excellent source for information on corporate officers and directors.

A clear advantage to researching media industries and companies today is found in the number of available electronic resources provided for users. Again, Appendix A offers a complete listing of the major electronic resources. One of the most popular is *Compact Disclosure*, a resource available on CD-ROM. *Compact Disclosure* offers data on eleven hundred public companies, including annual report information such as the president's letter and management discussion, financial data, and stock and earnings estimates. Individual companies can be searched using the company name, the description of a particular business segment, and the SIC code. Users have a number of options in retrieving information; you can download information to your own computer or simply print the information desired.

Market Concentration

Identifying the number of players in a given market will help to determine the type of market structure in which the firms are engaged. But remember that market structure does not necessarily explain how concentrated individual markets may be. Market concentration is an important variable in evaluating media markets. Highly concentrated markets usually lead to strong barriers to entry for new competitors. Historically, regulators have frowned on heavily concentrated markets, as evidenced by the policies of the Federal Communications Commission (FCC) on media ownership.

There are several different tools to measure different aspects of concentration in a market. To determine buyer concentration from the perspective of the audience, one can review the latest audience ratings or circulation data. In evaluating a market media, economists are usually interested in two other forms of concentration: concentration of ownership and concentration of market share (measured by revenue or some other variable).

Concentration of ownership. Concentration of ownership refers to the degree to which an industry is controlled by individual firms. Again, careful definition of the market under study is needed. Bagdikian (1993) documents a continuing decline in the number of firms involved in the media industries based on a variety of different factors. This trend will become more evident as you review later chapters that examine individual media industries. Concentration of ownership is considered problematic for society if it leads to a decline in diversity of expression.

The mass media are a critical force in helping to promote an informed electorate. Critics (Schiller, 1981) contend that as the media become more concentrated and less competitive, they not only have economic power, but political power as well, through the control and dissemination of information. As such, regulators attempt to limit concentration of control in order to maintain a diverse presentation of different views.

Concentration of market share. Different methods are used to measure the concentration of market share within a particular industry. One approach, mentioned briefly in Chapter 3, involves calculating *concentration ratios.* This measure of concentration compares the ratio of total revenues of the major players with the revenues of the entire industry, using the top four firms (CR4) or the top eight firms (CR8). If the four-firm ratio is equal to or greater than 50 percent, or if the eight-firm ratio is equal to or greater than 75 percent, then the market is considered highly concentrated (see Fig. 4-1).

Concentration ratios are best used to analyze trends over time. If the concentration ratio increases, this suggests a move toward monopolistic power. One problem with concentration ratios should be noted: the ratios themselves are not sensitive to the individual power held by single firms (Picard, 1989). For example, two different television markets may have identical concentration ratios, but the shares within the individual markets for each of the firms are very different. As Figure 4-2 illustrates, the distribution of market share is equal among the top four firms in market A, but in market B, the top firm clearly dominates the other three competitors.

	Top Four Firms	Top Eight Firms
High concentration	≥ 50%	≥ 75%
Moderate concentration	33% ≤ to < 50%	50% ≤ to < 75%
Low concentration	≤ 33%	≤ 50%

FIGURE 4-1. *Concentration ratios.*

Market A		Market B	
Firm 1	10	Firm 1	25
Firm 2	10	Firm 2	5
Firm 3	10	Firm 3	5
Firm 4	10	Firm 4	5

FIGURE 4-2. *Inequality in concentration ratios.*

The top-four and top-eight ratios have been frequently used to measure concentration in the media industries. An early study by Owen, Beebe and Manning (1974) found the market for television programs to be concentrated. Picard (1988) examined the newspaper industry using daily papers in local markets and found high concentration. Chan-Olmsted and Litman (1988) found that cable systems were moving toward concentration, although the ratios did not suggest that the market was highly concentrated.

Concentration can also be assessed graphically through the use of the *Lorenz Curve.* The Lorenz Curve illustrates the inequality of market share among different firms. Suppose one wishes to illustrate the fact that FM radio stations are the preferred choice over AM stations among listeners. An examination of a recent ratings book for a radio market finds 10 stations—five AM and five FM—competing for the audience in a particular time period. The five FM stations account for 82 percent of the radio audience, whereas the poor AM stations together only capture the remaining 18 percent. If audience shares were equally divided, then each station should have 10 percent of the audience. Thus, the FM stations should have only captured 50 percent of the market; however, because the FM stations reached far more than that, inequality exists.

The Lorenz Curve for the data in this example is illustrated in Figure 4-3. The 45° line represents equality in the market; the curve represents the actual distribution of shares among the radio stations. The more the Lorenz Curve departs from the 45° line, the greater the inequality. The utility of the Lorenz Curve lies in its graphical presentation, but it can be difficult to interpret

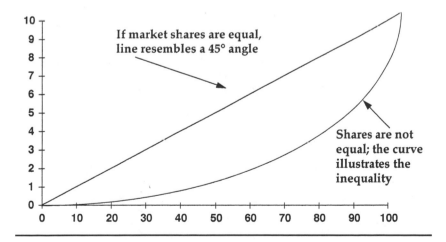

FIGURE 4-3. *Lorenz Curve.*

(Litman, 1985). It is best used when the number of firms in a market is greater than four.

A final measure of concentration, and probably the most sophisticated, is the Herfindahl-Hirschman Index (HHI). The HHI is calculated by summing the squared market shares of all firms in a given market. The index is considered more accurate than either concentration ratios or the Lorenz Curve in that the index increases as the number of firms declines and as inequality among individual firms rise. If the HHI equals 1,800 or higher, then a market is highly concentrated. If the index is less than 1,000, the market is considered un-concentrated (see Fig. 4-4). Calculating the HHI may be tedious if there are a large number of firms operating in a particular market.

The HHI has been used in several studies to measure media concentration, particularly in regards to network program categories. An earlier study by Litman (1979) used the HHI and found high concentration among program categories for the broadcast networks. Litman theorized that the data supported the proposition that the networks operate interdependently in an oligopolistic structure, rather than attempt to present a balanced program schedule.

The advantage of these three methods to measure concentration is that they offer different ways to measure and analyze concentration in a given market. Although a particular market structure may seem obvious with some media industries, the concentration measures can clarify the extent to which one or more companies dominate a particular market.

Corporate Diversification

On a related note, it may be of interest to determine how heavily an individual media firm is involved in a particular market. This can be done by analyzing the diversification strategy of individual companies. *Diversification* is the extent to which a company draws revenues across different markets or business segments. Normally, companies that draw profits from more than one segment or division are believed to be better equipped to handle fluctuations in

High concentration	$HHI > 1,800$
Moderate concentration	$1,000 \leq HHI \leq 1,800$
Unconcentrated	$HHI \leq 1,000$

FIGURE 4-4. *Herfindahl-Hirschmann Index (HHI).*

the normal business cycle. Further, by drawing resources across different markets, the diversified company is also thought to be able to adapt more easily to changing environmental conditions.

In a case study of the broadcast television networks, Dimmick and Wallschlaeger (1986) developed an index to measure corporate diversification. The index is calculated by summing the squared revenues of each business segment, and then dividing that sum into one (see Fig. 4-5). The diversification (D) index ranges from a low of one (meaning profits are concentrated in one division) to a high equal to the number of divisions the firm operates. Thus, a firm with seven divisions would have a D range from one to seven, whereas a firm with three divisions would have a D range from one to three.

The D measure has also been used to study diversification practices by companies involved in the premium cable industry (Albarran and Porco, 1990). The D index is best used when studying a company over a particular time span, as opposed to a single-year measurement, to reflect more accurately the changes companies encounter over time in the normal business cycle.

The D measure can be calculated using financial data from a corporate annual report or from an electronic service such as *Compact Disclosure*. A disadvantage to the D measure is that many corporations lump some of their activities together, and thus the financial information does not reflect the actual differences that may exist within a business segment. Nevertheless, the D measure can provide another means to analyze individual firms with respect to how deeply they are involved in certain markets.

Financial Ratios and Market Performance

It is also useful to have a basic knowledge of financial ratios in order to evaluate the financial condition and performance of individual firms and industries involved in the media (see Fig. 4-6). Data used to calculate financial

$$D = \frac{1}{\sum_{i=1}^{n} pi^2}$$

FIGURE 4-5. *Diversification index.* (Dimmick and Wallschlaeger, 1986)

Growth Ratios	measure growth over time
Performance Ratios	measure financial strength
Liquidity Ratios	convert assets into cash
Debt Ratios	measure debt and leverage
Capitalization	used in stock valuation

FIGURE 4-6. *Types of financial ratios.*

ratios can be found in several sources such as corporate annual reports. Additionally, some resources such as *Compact Disclosure* and *Standard & Poor's Industry Surveys* include a number of financial ratios as part of their overview of individual firms and industries.

Different types of ratios are used to gauge different types of performance. For example, *growth measures* calculate the growth of revenue and assets over time, and also document historical trends. Financial growth is important to any business, and the stronger these measures, the better for the firm or industry examined. These include growth of revenue, operating income, assets and net worth. For each growth measure, the previous time period (month, quarter or year) is subtracted from the current time period (month, quarter or year), and this number is divided by the previous time period.

Performance or profitability measures are designed to measure the financial strength of a company or industry. Low profitability measures are indications of high liabilities, low revenues or excessive expenses. Included in this set of measures are return on sales, return on assets, return on equity, price-earnings ratio and profit margins.

Other ratios are used to measure liquidity, debt and capitalization. Liquidity refers to a firm's ability to convert assets into cash. *Liquidity ratios* include the quick ratio, the current ratio and the acid-test ratio. Ideally, liquidity measures produce at least a 1.5-to-1 ratio of assets to liabilities. *Debt ratios* measure the debt of a firm or industry. The leverage ratio is calculated by dividing total debt by total assets. The lower the number the better. Another common debt measure is the debt-to-equity ratio, which divides total debt by total equity. Ideally, the debt-to-equity ratio will be no larger than one. *Capitalization ratios* are concerned with the capital represented by both preferred and common stock. Two ratios are common: dividing preferred stock by common stock and dividing long-term liabilities by common stock. Appendix B lists the formulas for the most commonly used financial ratios used by analysts to evaluate media firms and industries.

Impact of Regulation

All media firms and industries are to some degree affected by governmental regulation. The most obvious form of economic regulation concerns taxation; governments levy different taxes on corporations, but may also enact policies either to influence a particular market or to promote social goals. Some media industries are greatly influenced by regulation, though others face little regulation. For example, the FCC currently limits ownership of broadcast stations for both television and radio. On the other hand, local governments specify the franchise area for a cable system, but place no restrictions on newspaper distribution.

Media industries attempt to limit the impact of governmental regulation by forming industry associations, such as the National Association of Broadcasters (NAB) or the Newspaper Association of America (NAA). One way to circumvent potential governmental regulation is to provide self-regulation; industry associations often take the lead in this effort. Trade associations are also involved with professional lobbyists to attempt to sway regulators to their point of view.

As you investigate later chapters that focus on individual industries, you will discover that some industries face more regulatory challenges than others. Regulation may have both positive and negative outcomes in regards to media economics. As such, it is important to understand the desired goals regulators hope to achieve through regulation, and how those goals impact supply and demand curves, market structure, conduct and performance.

For example, the Telecommunications Act of 1996 will spur competition between cable systems, local phone companies and long-distance carriers. It will lead to radical changes in the way many households receive information and entertainment content. Consumers will likely have a choice of services, some of which may be close substitutes for one another, whereas others may be quite different. How much will consumers be willing to pay for such things as interactive shopping, banking and games? How will new services impact demand for existing technologies such as broadcast television? Competition may lead to an increase in suppliers and buyers, and lower consumer costs. On the other hand, it may cause some suppliers to exit a particular market if they are unable to achieve enough market share.

It is important to understand how regulation impacts media industries, and an analysis of the regulatory environment and the potential for future regulation is an important consideration in the evaluation of any particular media market. Monitoring the regulatory climate is an ongoing task in many media industries.

Impact of Technology

Like regulation, the mass media is affected by advances in technology. In the analysis of media markets, an effort should be made to understand the role technology plays in a particular industry. Technological change occurs rapidly in the communication industries. Like regulatory change, advances in technology can have both positive and negative outcomes. High-tech, automated equipment such as robotic-operated television cameras can operate flawlessly, but they also displace human camera operators. Satellite-delivered radio formats provide professional quality radio in many smaller markets, but at the same time, reduce a station's work force to a handful of employees.

From an economic standpoint, changes in technology will likely mean increases in equipment expenditures. When the newspaper industry moved from the old Linotype press to computerized layout and design, it resulted in massive purchases of new equipment. In covering television news, a continuing transition from film to video tape to instant coverage of events via satellite and microwave transmission has taken place in the last thirty years. In short, media industries must maintain efficient and modern methods to produce and distribute their content products with the highest possible quality.

The impact of technology must also be considered from the standpoint of the consumer. The decision by recording companies to invest heavily in the compact disc (CD) as the latest format for sound recordings was based in part on the fact that consumers would want the higher quality sound delivered by a digital audio system. However, this also drove up the cost for individual recordings and conversion to CD-based systems. Fiber optics and digital compression techniques can provide a television world of over five hundred channels of content, yet many users may only prefer a handful of channels.

The mass media are technologically driven industries and are heavily influenced by technological revolution. From an economic perspective, media industries should be examined in terms of their technical efficiency, as well as their ability to produce media content of consistently high technical quality. Technology should also be evaluated based on its ability to enhance a particular market, as well as the cost of implementing new technologies. Later chapters examine industries where technological change is most likely and how it may affect market performance.

Summary

This chapter summarizes different approaches used in evaluating media markets. This information enables you to understand the intricate processes at work in media economics among buyers and sellers. The ability to evaluate media markets is also important if you desire to invest in some part of the mass media, or if your professional goal is to gain employment in the mass media. Overall, a better understanding of the relationship between media and society and how economic factors impact that relationship is gained.

Evaluating a media industry first involves defining a particular market, which can be a difficult task. Careful examination and precise definitions are needed to clarify a particular market. A second step involves a process of determining what major companies are engaged in a particular market. Several reference resources are available to help in this process. Third, media markets should be evaluated in terms of the level of concentration that exists in the market. Different means of measuring concentration were introduced in this chapter, including concentration ratios, the Lorenz Curve, and the Herfindahl-Hirschman Index.

The chapter also introduced tools to examine individual companies, including an index of corporate diversification and a discussion of relevant financial ratios. The indices and ratios presented in the chapter offer different ways to interpret the economic viability of individual firms and industries.

All media industries are affected by regulation to some degree. Regulators use different goals for different industries, and regulations impact market structure, conduct and performance. Many industries attempt to minimize the impact of regulation by the presence of trade associations and lobbying efforts. Technology drives much of the mass media, and the impacts of technology must be examined in regards to how technology can affect market economics and performance, the pool for labor and talent in the media, and how consumers respond to new technology. As with regulation, technology can have both positive and negative impacts on media markets.

Understanding the criteria used in evaluating media industries presented in this chapter provides for a more comprehensive analysis of media markets and industries. Later chapters utilize this information in discussing specific media industries.

Discussion Questions

1. In order to analyze a media market, we must first define a market. How do we define a media market?

2. What are some of the different resources one can use to find out information about media industries? About media companies?
3. Discuss the different types of concentration. What tools can we use to measure concentration of market share?
4. What is corporate diversification? How is it measured?
5. Discuss different types of financial ratios used to analyze firms and industries. What do the ratios tell us? How can they be used?
6. Why is regulation used in the media industries? What is the purpose for regulation?
7. How does technology affect the mass media? How does technology affect society?

Exercises

1. Find a media industry you are interested in researching, using *Standard & Poor's Industry Surveys*. Using the financial information on the firms listed in your industry, calculate the top four and top eight concentration ratios (if there are eight firms) and the HHI Index for your industry. Is your industry concentrated? Explain.
2. Obtain a copy of a corporate annual report for a media company you are interested in. Using the materials presented in this text and the financial data in the corporate report, calculate a diversification index and at least three different ratios (growth, performance, liquidity, etc.) for the company. What does this information tell you about the company?
3. Review a recent trade magazine for an industry you are interested in (e.g., *Broadcasting and Cable*, *Editor and Publisher*, *Radio and Records*) and look for articles dealing with current or pending regulation. What did you learn from your research?
4. Using the same trade magazine, look for articles that discuss new or anticipated advances in technology. What does the article suggest as to how the new technology may impact the industry? What, if anything, does it say about how the technology may impact society?

References

Albarran, A. B. and Porco, J. (1990). Measuring and analyzing diversification of corporations involved in pay cable. *Journal of Media Economics,* 3(2):3–14.
Bagdikian, B. H. (1993). *The Media Monopoly,* 4th ed. Boston: Beacon Press.
Bates, B. J. (1993). Concentration in local television markets. *Journal of Media Economics* 6:3–22.
Chan-Olmsted, S. and Litman, B. R. (1988). Antitrust and horizontal mergers in the cable industry. *Journal of Media Economics* 1:63–74.
Dimmick, J. and Wallschlaeger, M. (1986). Measuring corporate diversification: A case study of new media ventures by television network parent companies. *Journal of Broadcasting and Electronic Media,* 30(1):1–14.
Litman, B. R. (1979). The television networks, competition and program diversity.

Journal of Broadcasting 23:393–410.

Litman, B. R. (1985). Economic methods of broadcasting research. In: Dominick, J. R. and Fletcher, J. E. (eds.). *Broadcasting Research Methods.* Boston: Allyn & Bacon, pp. 107–122.

Owen, B. M., Beebe, J. H., and Manning, W. G. (1974). *Television Economics.* Lexington, MA: D. C. Heath.

Picard, R. G. (1988). Measures of concentration in the daily newspaper industry. *Journal of Media Economics* 1:61–74.

Picard, R. G. (1989). *Media Economics.* Beverly Hills: Sage.

Schiller, H. I. (1981). *Who knows: Information in the Age of the Fortune 500.* Norwood, NJ: Random House.

*The
Broadcast
and
Cable
Industries*

5

THE RADIO INDUSTRY

In this chapter you will:

- Identify the major players, market structure and economic characteristics of the radio industry.

- Identify major trends that affected the growth of the radio industry.

- Learn how duopolies and local marketing agreements are changing the structure and conduct of the radio industry.

The radio industry is the oldest of the electronic media industries in the United States, with roots dating back to the mid-1800s, when numerous inventors attempted to transmit the early dots and dashes of Morse code through the air. Eventually, the trials and tribulations of these early pioneers would harness the technology in order to create radio transmitters and receivers. By the 1920s, the new medium of radio would capture the imagination and attention of the American public and fundamentally change the way society consumes information and entertainment (Matelski, 1993).

Seven decades later, the radio industry is still attracting audiences. The industry has changed considerably since KDKA, the first officially licensed radio station, broadcast the national election returns of 1920 to a handful of households in Pittsburgh. Today, over 9,600 commercial stations operate in the United States, reaching an estimated 77 percent of the total population every day (*Radio Marketing Guide and Factbook for Advertisers*, 1993–94).

Throughout its history, the radio industry has been forced to change and adapt as various social, technological and regulatory trends have affected the economic viability of the industry. A discussion of the entire history of the radio industry is beyond the scope of this chapter. However, five trends illustrate the resilient qualities of the radio industry: advertising, the development of networks, FM broadcasting, the advent of television, and the duopoly ownership rules. These trends are discussed in the following paragraphs.

Advertising. The sale of time for advertising purposes, or "toll broadcasting" as it was originally called, began in 1922 on WEAF, New York, a station owned at the time by AT&T (Barnouw, 1966). The ability of radio to attract local advertisers who desired access to audiences gave the nascent radio industry an economic base from which to grow. Prior to the use of advertising, the only way that radio stations made money was through the sale of radio receivers. Many of the early companies involved in radio station ownership (e.g., Westinghouse, General Electric, American Marconi) also manufactured radio receivers. Advertising gave radio stations another source of revenue, which would be much more lucrative than the sale of radio sets. In time, advertising would develop into national and regional, as well as local, markets.

Network development. By the mid-1920s, radio stations were in a scramble for programming. Most of the early programming was live, and many stations operated only limited hours. The Radio Corporation of America (RCA), the electronics giant that was formed primarily to manufacture and sell radio receivers, developed a programming service that could be linked to other radio stations around the country. Not surprisingly, RCA hoped that the new service would sell more radio sets. In 1926, the NBC radio network debuted to provide programming to its affiliated stations (Head, Sterling and Schofield, 1994). A year later, the Columbia Broadcasting System (CBS) began operation. In later years, NBC would expand by developing an additional network (renamed the NBC "red" and the "blue" networks). The growth of networks created a national market for radio, enabling advertisers to reach large audiences across the nation. The practice of networking stabilized the industry and created a common culture in society. Radio networks still exist today, although the programming primarily consists of news and feature materials.

FM. After years of experimentation, FM (frequency modulation) broadcasting began in 1941 (Matelski, 1993). The FM signal quality was superior to the AM (amplitude modulation) signals, although the audience shift to FM from AM would be very slow. By 1978, the FM radio audience outnumbered the AM audience for the first time. Since then, FM radio has dominated the radio industry, with AM listening now accounting for less than 25 percent of the total time spent listening to radio. FM stations typically rank as the most profitable stations in most radio markets.

The advent of television. Television's emergence from the post-war years of the 1940s to the rapid growth in the 1950s brought considerable hardships to the radio industry. Popular programs and performers, along with the advertisers who sponsored them, made the transition from radio to the new visual television medium. And as programs, performers and advertisers left radio, so did the audience—especially during prime-time hours. The radio industry was forced to adapt. No longer the primary distributor of national programming and advertising, the radio industry recognized that in order to survive it had to rely on the local market for economic support. Radio stations began to differentiate themselves by adopting different formats, such as Top 40, country, middle-of-the-road, and news/talk in order to appeal to different audiences and local advertisers targeting those audiences.

Duopoly rules. Prior to 1992, no group or individual could own more than one AM or one FM station in a single market. This Federal Communications Commission (FCC) provision, known as the duopoly rule, was designed to prevent concentration of ownership in local markets. A single owner could now own up to four stations in large markets (defined as markets with 15 or more stations), and as many as three stations in smaller markets, no more than two of which may be the same service class (Barrett, 1993). The 1992 rules encouraged economies of scale and efficiency in the radio industry through the combining of existing operations. As will be seen later in this chapter, duopolies are on the rise across the radio industry.

These trends illustrate some of the major changes the radio industry has encountered over the years. Today, the radio industry is enjoying a resurgence following the sluggish performance of the early 1990s, when many radio stations suffered severe losses due to the economic recession.

The Radio Market

The contemporary radio industry consists of different markets operating simultaneously. The local market represents the geographic area or region where local radio stations target listeners and advertisers. And within each local market, smaller submarkets can be found, such as the submarket for a particular type of listener (in terms of demographic qualities) or the submarket for those stations carrying a similar type of format.

For example, your author resides in the Dallas–Fort Worth radio market, currently ranked as the seventh largest radio market (in terms of population) in the United States. In the Dallas–Fort Worth radio market, one can tune in to approximately 40 radio signals (see Table 5-1). In one sense, all of the stations compete against one another for listeners and advertisers. However, as learned in Chapter 4, this simplistic approach presents an inaccurate view of the radio market, as these stations differ in format, technical characteristics and demographic targets.

Country stations in the Dallas–Fort Worth market include KSCS, KPLX, KYNG and WBAP, and each station offers a slightly different demographic profile of its listeners, most of whom are male. If the market desired is African-American males, radio stations such as KJMZ, KKDA and KHVN represent

Table 5 1. AM and FM radio stations in the Dallas Fort Worth market

Network	Format
AM	
KPYK	Big band/easy listening
KGGR	Black Christian
KDFT	Black gospel
KHVN	Black gospel
KAHZ	Children's music
KSKY	Christian, talk, music
KPBC	Christian country
KBEC	Classic country
KGBS	CNN News, talk
KGVL	Country
KDMM	'40s, '50s, and '60s hits
KMRT	Mexican Top 40
WBAP	News/talk
KRLD	News/talk
KKDA	Soul, gospel, talk
KESS	Spanish
KFJZ	Spanish
KRVA	Spanish
KXEB	Spanish
KTNO	Spanish religious
KTCK	Sports talk
KLIF	Talk/NBC
KICI	Tejano music
FM	
KDMX	Adult contemporary
KEOM	Adult contemporary
KVIL	Adult contemporary
KXGM	Adult contemporary
KTXQ	Album rock
KLTY	Christian
WRR	Classical
KZPS	Classic rock
KNON	Community
KYNG	Contemporary country
KHKS	Contemporary hits
KEMM	Country
KIKT	Country
KSCS	Country
KSNN	Country
KPLX	Country
KDZR	Hard rock
KCBI	Inspirational
KTCU	Jazz/alt. rock
KNTU	Jazz, classical
KERA	National Public Radio, eclectic
KDGE	New rock
KLUV	Oldies
KETR	Oldies, jazz
KVTT	Religious
KEGL	Rock
KRRW	Rock 'n' roll oldies

Table 5-1. Continued

Network	Format
KOAI	Smooth jazz
KRVA	Spanish
KTLR	Tejano and classic country
KCYT	Tejano music
KICI	Tejano music
KJMZ	Urban contemporary
KKDA	Urban contemporary

competitors. On the other hand, if advertisers want to reach listeners with incomes over $75,000 a year, then KLIF, KRLD and WRR form a logical submarket.

A second market that prevails in the radio industry is the national market. There are two possible ways to define the national radio market. One is by the total number of listeners reached on a national basis by radio group operators (see Table 5-2). You will recognize several familiar names on this list, including CBS and Capital Cities/ABC. The listing of the top 25 radio groups is in a constant state of flux due to mergers and duopolies (Zier, 1993 and 1994).

Another way to define the national radio market is by the national radio networks. There are approximately twenty-five radio networks, which together

Table 5-2. Radio industry group owners (1994)

Group	Number of Stations
Bonneville	17
CapCities/ABC	21
CBS	39
Chancellor	33
Clear Channel	36
Cox	15
Emmis	5
Evergreen	34
EZ Communications	14
Gannett	13
Great American	13
Greater Media	11
Infinity	27
Inner City Broadcasting	5
Jacor	19
Jefferson-Pilot Comm.	13
Nationwide	11
Secret Communications	14
Susquehanna	16
Tribune Broadcasting	6
Viacom	12

form a market that serves national advertisers and individual radio stations. The major national radio networks are listed in Table 5-3. Some of these networks provide specific types of news, features and other programs, whereas other networks provide a full, 24-hour schedule of programming. All of the national radio networks are fed by satellite to their affiliates. The market share of the national radio networks can be measured by the number of stations that are affiliated with each network, by the number of listeners each service can reach, or by the amount of advertising dollars each network generates.

Demand in the radio industry. There are three major types of demand observable in the radio industry: demand by consumers, demand by advertisers, and demand for the stations themselves by potential owners and investors. Here, we focus on the demand by consumers and advertisers. The demand for stations will be discussed later in the chapter.

Table 5-3. Examples of radio networks

ABC Radio Networks:
    ABC Contemporary
    ABC Direction
    ABC Entertainment
    ABC FM
    ABC Information
    ABC Rock
    ABC Talk
    ESPN Radio Network
    Satellite Music Network

American Urban Radio Networks:
    American Urban Radio Network
    SBN Sports Network
    STRZ Entertainment Network

CBS Radio Networks:
    CBS Hispanic Radio Network
    CBS News Radio
    CBS Radio Network
    CBS Spectrum

Unistar:
    CNN Radio
    Unistar
    Unistar Power
    Unistar Super
    Unistar Ultimate

Westwood One Radio Networks:
    NBC Talknet
    Westwood Mutual
    Westwood NBC
    Westwood Source
    Westwood W.O.N.E.

Consumer demand is best indicated by statistics generated by the radio industry. According to the Radio Advertising Bureau (1993–94), 99 percent of all households have a radio, with an average of 5.6 radios per household. Radios are also found in 95 percent of all automobiles. Radio reaches an estimated 95 percent of all persons ages 12 and up each week, with each individual averaging 3 hours and 20 minutes of listening.

One of the fastest growing areas in the radio industry is Hispanic radio stations. The growth of the Hispanic population has increased demand for stations catering to Hispanic audiences. Advertisers have also added to the demand, needing radio to help market products to Hispanic listeners. According to Gerlin (1993), Hispanic radio stations have increased 21 percent since 1990, and advertising on these stations has grown at an annual rate of 5.5 percent.

Overall, radio advertising revenues have grown steadily. Table 5-4 lists radio revenues from selected years in the categories of local, spot (national advertising on local stations) and network advertising. Several trends are observable. First, total radio revenues more than doubled from 1980 ($3.541 billion) to 1990 ($8.839 billion). Second, local ad revenues remain the most important, followed by spot and network. Third, revenues for 1993 rebounded strongly from the recession years of 1991 and 1992 to reach an all-time high of $9.57 billion (Standard & Poor's, 1994). Veronis, Suhler and Associates (1994) projects radio advertising revenues will grow at an annual rate of 7.1 percent by 1998 to reach $13.2 billion.

Major Players in the Radio Industry

Federal regulations, historically, have limited the number of radio stations a single group or individual could own. The passage of the Telecommunications

Table 5-4. Radio advertising revenues (billions of dollars)

Year	Local	Spot	Network	Total
1980	$ 2,643	$ 740	$ 158	$ 3,541
1985	4,915	1,319	329	6,563
1986	5,313	1,333	380	7,026
1987	5,605	1,315	371	7,292
1988	6,109	1,402	382	7,893
1989	6,463	1,530	427	8,420
1990	6,780	1,626	433	8,839
1991	6,578	1,573	440	8,591
1992	6,899	1,479	388	8,766
1993	7,526	1,627	407	9,560
1994	8,370	1,860	411	10,650

Source: Adapted from *Radio Marketing Guide and Factbook for Advertisers* (1993–94) and other sources compiled by the author.

Act of 1996 removed all national ownership limits in the radio industry, while maintaining caps on local ownership in individual markets. In short, the larger the market the more stations an individual or company may own.

For example, in markets with 45 or more commercial stations, a single company may own up to eight stations with no more than five in a single class (AM or FM). If the market has 30–44 stations, the number drops to a total of seven, with a maximum of four in the same class. For markets with 15–29 stations, the numbers drop to a total of six and four of a kind; in markets with 14 or fewer stations, the number drops to five and no more than three of a kind (or up to half the stations in the market).

Consolidation will continue to increase in the radio industry now that national ownership caps have been removed. As Table 5-2 illustrates, the top five companies in the radio industry are CBS, Clear Channel, Evergreen, Chancellor and Infinity. As for national radio networks, Disney-owned Capital Cities/ABC leads the industry through its seven network divisions and its eleven national formats available through ABC/Satellite Music Networks. Other leaders in the radio network market include Unistar, Mutual, and CBS.

Market Structure

In terms of market structure, monopolistic competition best describes the radio industry at both the local and national levels. Recall that a monopolistic competitive market structure exists when there are many sellers offering products that are similar, but not perfect, substitutes for one another. Such is the case with radio. At the local level, several stations may program the same type of format, but the style of the air staff, technical facilities, program formatics and listener appeal will distinguish stations from one another. Further, each radio station or network attempts to differentiate their on-air product in the mind of the listener through different promotion and marketing strategies. Consider the radio stations in the area where you are reading this chapter. How do the stations attempt to distinguish themselves from other stations? What tactics are used in your local market?

Future changes in ownership limits and duopoly requirements could gradually shift the radio industry from a monopolistic competitive market structure toward oligopoly. However, regulators have been historically conservative when considering increases in ownership limits to prevent increasing concentration of control. At present, market structure in the radio industry is best described as monopolistic competition.

Market Concentration

Market concentration measures in the radio industry routinely indicate low levels of concentration in the national market. Market share is usually measured by first totaling all 12-and-older listeners from 6 a.m. to midnight, Sunday through Monday, for each station, and then adding station groups together. In analyzing the impact of duopoly rules on radio station ownership, Chan-Olmsted (in press) observed a trend toward greater concentration using the ratios of the top four firms (CR4) and the top eight firms (CR8), but well below the benchmarks used to indicate concentrated markets. Between 1992 and 1993, the CR4 share dropped from 11 percent to 7.1 percent, whereas the top eight firms increased from 5.7 percent to 10.6 percent. Chan-Olmsted theorized that the revised duopoly rules may lead to further shifts in ownership among the top and middle markets, with more concentration of control likely.

In measuring concentration in the radio industry, the CR4 and CR8 ratios offer the easiest interpretation, particularly in local radio markets. The Herfindahl-Hirschman Index (HHI) can be used as well, but in markets with a large number of stations, the calculations can be tedious and the results will usually indicate little concentration, as the squared market shares are likely to be very small.

Although measures of concentration typically indicate low levels of concentration in radio markets, barriers to entry are still rather formidable. In local markets, barriers to entry exist due to the lack of available frequencies for new stations. In the majority of geographical markets around the country, most of the available radio channels are taken by existing broadcasters. Thus, the only way to enter the market is through the acquisition of an existing station.

Demand for radio stations. Radio station sales during the period 1992 to 1994 are listed in Table 5-5. The number of transactions increased dramatically from 1992 to 1994, a direct impact of the duopoly rules. In 1992, a total of 208 AM stations were sold at an average price of $357,000 (excluding the sale of WFAN, New York, for $70 million). In 1993, the number of AM stations sold increased to 231, but the average price dropped to $311,294. For FM stations, a total of 289 stations changed hands at an average price of $882,000; by 1993, some 402 stations were sold at an average price of $1,849,604—an increase of nearly 110 percent. Keep in mind that these are average prices—meaning that in larger markets, the sale of a radio station can reach millions of dollars. In 1994, sales of AM stations totaled $132.3 million, and FM sales totaled $838 million. At the time of publication, the record for a single station is Infinity's purchase of KRTH-FM, Los Angeles, for $110 million.

The high prices for radio stations, and the added monthly expenses for payroll, programming and other resources, form considerable financial barriers to entry for new competitors in the radio industry. Entering the radio industry will likely become more expensive in the years ahead as consolidation continues.

Table 5-5. Radio station transactions (AM/FM breakdown 1992–94)

	AM		FM	
Year	Number of Transactions	Average Station Price	Number of Transactions	Average Station Price
1992	208	$ 357,000	289	$ 882,000
1993	231	311,294	402	1,849,604
1994	169	782,840	310	2,703,225

Source: Compiled from industry trade sources and Federal Communications Commission data.

Government Regulation

Because radio stations are licensed by the federal government through the FCC, certain policies must be adhered to by all stations. Deregulation of the radio industry during the 1970s and 1980s eliminated many bureaucratic requirements for the industry, but several important policies remain. For example, radio stations must apply for renewal of their licenses every eight years in order to continue broadcasting. On an annual basis, stations must file employment reports with the FCC to show compliance with equal employment opportunity guidelines. And on a daily basis, stations must have operators on duty who carry restricted permits, maintain a public file of station information for inspection by local citizens, and monitor and maintain technical facilities (transmitter power, operational tower lights, etc.).

The changes in the duopoly rules, initiated in 1992, have been one of the more significant regulatory decisions to impact the radio industry in recent years. Between September 1992 and June 1994, the FCC received 935 applications for duopoly operations (Petrozzello, 1994b). Duopoly has strengthened the radio industry by enabling operators (a) to combine operations in order to lower costs, and (b) to market up to four different stations to advertisers and audiences. Duopoly has some disadvantages as well, the most obvious being the elimination of jobs as stations are combined.

Another ruling enacted at the same time as the duopoly rule was the approval for stations to program and market other stations through *local marketing agreements*, or LMAs. In an LMA, a station agrees to allow a stronger station to provide some of the programming and sell advertising. In an LMA, the ownership of the brokered station does not change, as it does in a duopoly. The FCC has established limits on the amount of program material that may be duplicated (25 percent), as well as the amount of time that may be sold (no more than 15 percent) on the brokered station (Barrett, 1993). A total of 335 LMA applications were filed with the FCC from September 1992 through May 1994 (Petrozzello, 1994a).

Radio station ownership limits have changed several times since 1984. In 1984, an owner was limited to no more than seven AM and seven FM stations. The deregulatory environment during the Reagan administration led to changes in 1985, when the FCC adopted the "12–12 rule," which increased ownership to 24 stations. In 1992, the limits were increased again to 18 and 18, or 36 total. In September 1994, the limit rose to 20 and 20 (Petrozzello, 1994b). The structure of the radio industry will continue to change dramatically now that national ownership limits have been removed with the passage of the Tele-communications Act of 1996. The larger markets will likely move toward an oligopolistic structure given the rapid pace of mergers and acquisitions observed in the radio industry in recent years.

Technological Forces Affecting Radio

Dramatic changes could be in store for the radio industry with the deployment of digital equipment to create a third class of radio service, digital audio broadcasting (DAB). The technology for DAB is evolving. The problem is the costs associated to implement DAB (Scully, 1993). With the radio industry continuing to attract listeners and advertisers through traditional analog broadcasting, there is no real need by the industry to launch a DAB service, even though the sound quality would be vastly superior to existing AM and FM stations. Radio owners and managers are also concerned that a DAB service would be detrimental to existing AM and FM radio stations by siphoning the listening audience (Ducey, 1993).

The radio industry will also be impacted by the development of the "electronic superhighway," which will merge program suppliers and the telephone, broadcast and computer industries. Radio will likely have a role in the electronic superhighway, although it is yet to be determined. One possibility is the creation and expansion of existing networks and programming material, which could then be accessed or stored in home computer systems.

The Economic Future of Radio

As the oldest of the electronic media, the radio industry has adapted throughout history to various forces that have affected its economic potential. In every case, the radio industry has not only survived, but actually has been strengthened. Today, the radio industry is a mature industry, but it continues to have a promising future.

Advertising revenue is expected to rise faster for the radio industry than for the television industry through 1998 (Veronis, Suhler and Associates, 1994). Radio remains an efficient advertising buy when compared with other media (*Radio Marketing Guide and Factbook for Advertisers*, 1993–94), and is particularly useful in targeting specific demographic groups through various program formats.

AM radio, which has lost audience since 1978, has been rejuvenated by a host of syndicated talk shows (e.g., Rush Limbaugh, Howard Stern, Don Imus, Gordon Liddy) who have brought listeners back to the medium (Lewis, 1993; Petrozzello, 1994a). FM radio continues to hold audiences with a variety of music formats, and radio networks have expanded over the past decade to include 24-hour packaged formats and a range of feature programs and news.

The 1992 duopoly/LMA rulings, along with a further easing of ownership limits, have spurred new investment in the radio industry. Weaker stations have benefited through duopoly/LMA arrangements, and stronger stations have expanded market share (Foisie, 1994). The prospects of new ways to deliver programming, through either DAB or the electronic superhighway, may mean additional revenue streams for the radio industry in the years ahead.

Summary

The radio industry is the oldest of the electronic media industries, and certainly the most resilient. The radio industry introduced and perfected the practices of advertising, networking and programming, which would form the basis of broadcasting. Over 9,600 commercial stations are in operation, reaching 99 percent of all households in the United States.

The radio industry operates in two distinct markets. At the local level, stations compete for local listeners and advertisers attracted to the programming formats used by each station. Nationally, radio networks compete for audiences and advertisers through news and programming services as well as 24-hour satellite-delivered formats.

Throughout the local and national markets, the radio industry reflects a monopolistic competitive structure. Measures of concentration indicate that the radio industry remains unconcentrated, although changes in ownership rules and relaxation of the old duopoly rule may lead to increasing concentration in the industry. Major players include CBS, Infinity, Capital Cities/ABC, Evergreen, and Chancellor.

In addition to the demand for radio by consumers and advertisers, there is also demand for the stations as investment properties. The high average prices for stations, coupled with the lack of open channels for broadcasting, create financial barriers of entry for new competitors in the industry.

Recent changes in regulation through the new duopoly rules and LMAs have renewed interest in radio as an investment. Relaxed ownership limits will raise the value of radio properties, as well as concentration in the industry. Digital audio broadcasting looms as a third form of radio service, but will be slow to develop due to costs.

Although the radio industry is a mature industry, estimates for advertiser demand through 1998 are expected to be strong at a projected 7 percent annual growth rate. With personalities like Rush Limbaugh, talk radio has flourished on AM radio and has slowed the erosion of listeners to FM. FM listenership remains strong as well. Further consolidation within the industry due to new duopolies and LMAs will continue to spur economic investment in the radio industry for the next several years. Overall, the radio industry continues to adapt and change, as it has throughout its colorful history.

Discussion Questions

1. How has radio changed over the years? What factors have impacted radio's economic development over time?
2. Discuss the types of markets in which the radio industry competes with other suppliers for audiences and advertisers.
3. How is demand observed in the radio industry? Discuss the types of demand and provide an example of each.
4. How have changes in radio ownership and the duopoly/LMA rules impacted the value of radio stations? What might happen in the future if ownership limits continue to be raised?

Exercises

1. Analyze the radio stations in the market in which you currently live by gathering the following information:
   a. Technical qualities of each station (class, power, etc.)
   b. Format of the station, call letters/logo
   c. Target audience
   d. Advertisers
   e. Promotion and marketing efforts to increase public awareness of each station.
2. Review local periodicals for your market for the past five years to determine how many radio stations have been sold, the price for each station and who is the new owner. Are any of the owners in your market found in Table 5-2?
3. Determine if any stations in your market are involved in either duopolies or LMAs. If possible, try to talk with a member of station management to determine how duopoly has affected the local market for radio.
4. Determine how many radio networks are present in your market, and write a brief summary of the programming presented by one of the networks. The network can be a news/programming service or it can be a satellite-delivered format.

References

Barnouw, E. (1966). *A Tower in Babel: A History of Broadcasting in the United States.* Volume I—to 1933. New York: Oxford University Press.

Barrett, A. C. (1993). Public policy and radio: A regulator's view. *Media Studies Journal* 7(3):139–150.

Chan-Olmsted, S. (in press). Deregulation of radio ownership rules: Analyzing the economic impact of duopoly. *Journal of Radio Studies.*

Ducey, R. V. (1993). Riding radio's technological wave. *Media Studies Journal* 7(3):151–158.

Foisie, G. (1994). Duopolies growing in revenue share. *Broadcasting & Cable,* March 21, p. 48.

Gerlin, A. (1993). Radio stations gain by going after Hispanics. *The Wall Street Journal,* July 14, pp. B1, B8.

Head, S. W., Sterling, C. H., and Schofield, L. B. (1994). *Broadcasting in America: A survey of Electronic Media,* 7th ed. Boston: Houghton Mifflin Company.

Lewis, T. (1993). Triumph of the idol: Rush Limbaugh and a hot medium. *Media Studies Journal* 7(3):51–62.

Matelski, M. J. (1993). Resilient radio. *Media Studies Journal* 7(3):1–13.

Petrozzello, D. (1994a). Syndication brings big names to smaller markets. *Broadcasting & Cable,* June 13, pp. 34–35.

Petrozzello, D. (1994b). Radio ownership limit inches up. *Broadcasting & Cable,* September 12, pp. 40–41.

Radio Advertising Bureau (1993–94). *Radio Marketing Guide and Factbook for Advertisers.* New York: Radio Advertising Bureau.

Scully, S. (1993). DAB: Radio's uncertain digital future. *Broadcasting & Cable,* September 6, p. 46.

Standard & Poor's (1994). *Standard & Poor's Industry Surveys.* New York: Standard & Poor's.

Veronis, Suhler and Associates (1994). *Communications Industry Forecast.* New York: Veronis, Suhler and Associates.

Zier, J. A. (1993). Station sales rebound in '93. *Broadcasting & Cable,* March 7, pp. 33–37.

Zier, J. A. (1994). Ranking TV and radio's top players. *Broadcasting & Cable,* March 21, pp. 52–56.

6

THE TELEVISION INDUSTRY

In this chapter you will:

- Identify the major players, market structure and economic characteristics of the television industry.

- Understand how networks engage in vertical integration and economies of scale.

- Recognize the different types of demand in the television industry.

- Understand the importance of advertising to the television industry.

- Recognize how regulatory decisions have previously limited, but currently favor, television industry economics.

Despite a continual assault from new forms of video entertainment for audiences and advertisers over the past twenty years, the broadcast television industry continues to dominate the electronic media landscape. The "big four" networks of ABC, CBS, NBC and Fox are the leaders of the television industry, operating in an interdependent relationship with local affiliates who carry much of the network programming schedule. The programming enables the networks to capture the majority of the viewers and the advertising dollars targeted for the television industry.

The television industry grew rapidly in the United States during the post-war years of the 1940s, thanks to its older sibling, the radio industry. As discussed in Chapter 5, the radio industry established and refined the practices of networking, programming and advertising that would easily adapt to the new television medium. By the mid-1950s, television had become the primary source of entertainment and information in most households and had established itself as a major influence on American culture.

Network television became such a powerful social and economic force that, by the early 1970s, a series of regulatory actions by Congress and the Federal Communications Commission (FCC) were enacted to stimulate competition in the television industry and to limit network power. In 1970, the networks were stripped of any meaningful financial interest in the lucrative syndication programming market for off-network series. The following year, the prime-time access rule (PTAR) was adopted to limit the number of hours of network programming in prime-time and to encourage more local programming. Later, cable television systems were cleared of hurdles that restricted the importation of distant signals in local television markets.

Regulatory actions and new competition from cable and the VCR resulted in a loss of market share for the television networks throughout the 1980s. Further competition came from independent television stations, whose position was strengthened by the growth of cable television. Independents suddenly achieved visual parity with network affiliates in cable households. Independents were also able to utilize off-network series during the access time period, as well as to showcase first-run syndication programs such as *Star Trek: The Next Generation.*

Larger chains of television stations were created following a 1985 FCC decision to allow TV owners to increase the number of stations they could own from seven to 12, or up to a maximum of 25 percent of the national television audience (Albarran, 1989). Included among these new chains was Fox Broadcasting Company, which acquired the former Metromedia television stations in 1986 and would later become the cornerstone for the Fox network. Other groups also grew in size and stature, including Paramount, Silver King (Home Shopping Club stations) and Univision (Spanish broadcasting).

Capital Cities Communications Inc. merged with ABC in 1986, the same year NBC and parent company RCA were acquired by General Electric (Auletta, 1991). CBS would undergo changes in its management structure in 1987, after fending off two hostile takeover attempts, including one from cable visionary Ted Turner (Auletta, 1991). In 1987, the Fox network officially became a "fourth" network, offering a limited prime-time schedule, which would later grow to include all seven nights by the start of the 1994 season.

Competition for audiences and advertisers continued to intensify, and the recessionary years of 1991-92 resulted in huge economic losses for the networks. Still, the networks were able to maintain at least a dominant share of the national television audience. In 1994, prime-time viewing of network affiliate stations was estimated at 72 percent across all television households (Nielsen Media Research, 1994).

Unrest in the television industry continues in the mid 1990s. Fox established itself as a formidable power in the television industry by securing the coveted National Football League's national conference (NFC) games, which had aired on CBS for years, and then by acquiring a number of stronger affiliates in several major markets (Jensen and Carnevale, 1994).

Fox added further upheaval in the television industry in May 1994 with the announcement that New World Communications would be switching all 12 of its television stations to the Fox network, secured by a $500 million investment from Fox. Ten of the 12 stations were in the top 50 markets and, in several markets, CBS, NBC and ABC were suddenly without affiliates. The announcement triggered a mad scramble during the summer of 1994 by all the networks to enter into long-term affiliation agreements to secure affiliate relations. Individual stations were able to negotiate stronger compensation payments as a result of Fox's move, improving their economic position.

Two new national broadcast networks began programming in January 1995: United/Paramount Network (UPN), a joint venture of the Chris-Craft and Paramount television stations, and Warner Brothers, a new network from Time Warner Entertainment. Like Fox, the new networks will enter the national network market with a limited prime-time schedule. Two major ownership changes at the network level took place in 1995. The Walt Disney Company acquired Capital Cities/ABC, while Westinghouse acquired CBS. The networks maintained their public identity as ABC and CBS respectively.

Much like the radio industry, the television industry has undergone a series of changes and transitions over the past 50 years. The television industry faces many challenges in the years ahead as it continues to encounter competition from new and expanded delivery systems. Economically, the television industry is equipped to maintain a strong leadership position in the competitive video marketplace.

The Television Market

The television industry consists of several different markets. At the local level, television stations (network affiliates, independents and public stations) compete with one another in the market for audiences, as well as with other close substitutes to the broadcast channels—most notably the cable channels (Bates, 1993). Commercial stations also compete with other stations and substitutes as a supplier of time for local advertisers. The number of competitors varies in local television markets depending on how many television channels are allocated to each market by the FCC. In general, larger markets were awarded a higher number of commercial television channels than were medium and small markets. The top 20 local television markets are listed in Table 6-1.

At the national level, the four broadcast networks also compete in a dual product marketplace for audiences and advertisers. Demand for audiences at the

Table 6 1. Top 20 television markets

Location	Rank	TV Households
New York	1	6,692,370
Los Angeles	2	5,006,380
Chicago	3	3,070,830
Philadelphia	4	2,661,360
San Francisco–Oakland–San Jose	5	2,253,220
Boston	6	2,104,900
Washington, DC	7	1,855,440
Dallas–Ft. Worth	8	1,816,700
Detroit	9	1,735,340
Houston	10	1,510,580
Atlanta	11	1,510,340
Cleveland	12	1,446,970
Seattle–Tacoma	13	1,427,750
Minneapolis–St. Paul	14	1,389,420
Tampa–St. Petersburg, Sarasota	15	1,384,150
Miami–Ft. Lauderdale	16	1,296,800
Pittsburgh	17	1,141,830
St. Louis	18	1,109,090
Sacramento–Stockton–Modesto	19	1,099,950
Phoenix	20	1,097,480

Source: Adapted from *Broadcasting and Cable Yearbook* (1994).

national level is assessed by audience ratings compiled by Nielsen Media Research and other industry sources. Advertiser demand is available from different sources, including advertising agencies and independent firms.

Consumer demand for television. According to Nielsen Media Research (1993–94), 98 percent of all households in the United States have at least one television, with 69 percent having more than one set. On an annual basis, these television sets are on an average of seven hours per day. Household viewing levels (referred to as households using television, or HUT) rise throughout the day for the television industry, and peak during the prime-time hours of 8 p.m.–11 p.m. Sunday evening is the most popular night for TV viewing, followed by Monday evening. The least popular nights for watching television are Friday and Saturday.

Nielsen Media Research (1993–94) reports that across all TV households, approximately 73 percent of the total viewing time is divided among the networks and their affiliate stations. This statistic is impressive given the many alternatives consumers now have through other forms of video entertainment and information.

Advertiser demand for television. Revenues from advertisers come from several different markets. At the national level, advertisers buy time from the networks in a two-step process. In the *upfront* market, advertising time is purchased during the early summer months for the upcoming fall season (Goldman, 1994). The networks want to sell as much of their inventory (spot purchases) as possible in the upfront market. For example, in 1994, over $4 billion of upfront advertising was sold by the networks (ABC, $1.35 billion; CBS, $1.2 billion; NBC $1.15 billion; Fox, $700 million). Unsold time is retained and offered during the television season; this market is called the *scatter* market. The scatter market functions throughout the television season.

At the local level, advertising is sold by local broadcast stations throughout the year. Local advertising is offered to local businesses, whereas national spot advertising is available for national advertisers who purchase time in local markets through various advertising agencies. Certain time periods are more lucrative than others for local stations. In particular, the "sweeps" months of February, May, July and November represent good opportunities for advertisers, as programmers offer their best products to the audience. Prices for advertising usually rise during the sweeps period as a result of high demand by local advertisers.

Advertising on television is a billion-dollar industry. Table 6-2 lists the advertising spent on television for selected years. Notice that network advertising has grown steadily since 1989, whereas local and spot advertising suffered during the recessionary years of 1991–92. Veronis, Suhler and Associates (1994) project television advertising at the network level will grow at a rate of 5.3 percent through 1998, compared with a growth rate of 5.6 percent for local stations, reaching a combined estimate of $34.7 billion.

Table 6-2. Television advertising (in millions)

Year	Network	Spot	Local	Total
1985	$ 8,285	$ 6,004	$ 5,714	$ 20,003
1987	8,500	6,846	6,833	22,179
1989	9,110	7,354	7,612	24,076
1990	9,565	7,905	7,875	25,345
1991	8,915	7,280	7,775	23,970
1992	10,332	7,551	8,080	25,963
1993*	11,033	8,004	8,816	27,853
1994*	11,585	8,150	9,200	28,935

Source: Robert Cohen, McCann-Erickson.
*Estimates by author.

Major Players in the Television Industry

As in the radio industry, FCC regulations limit the number of television stations a single group or individual may own. Television ownership is based on two criteria. First, no group or individual may own more than 12 stations. Second, an audience "reach cap" limits a single owner to 35 percent of the national audience. The reach cap is determined by totaling the percentage of television households available in each local market. Of the nation's more than fifteen hundred television stations, approximately 76 percent are commercial TV stations (By the numbers, 1994). Group owners dominate the television industry, with roughly 70 percent of all television stations owned by groups (Carroll and Davis, 1993). The major television group owners are listed in Table 6-3.

Table 6-3. Top 25 television group owners (1995)

Group	Rank	Number of Stations
A. H. Belo	13	7
Capital Cities/ABC*	1	8
CBS**	5	7
Chris Craft/United Television	7	8
Cox Enterprises	15	6
Disney*	23	1
Fox	2	12
Gannett	11	10
Group W(estinghouse)**	9	8
Hearst	17	6
Hubbard Broadcasting	21	9
Lin Broadcasting	18	9
NBC	3	6
New World	8	12
Paramount	22	6
Post-Newsweek	16	6
Providence Journal	24	11
Pulitzer	20	10
Renaissance	19	9
River City Broadcasting	25	7
Scripps Howard	14	9
Silver King Communications	6	12
Telemundo	12	6
Tribune Broadcasting	4	8
Univision	10	9

Source: McClellan (1995). Rank based on percentage of total audience reached by owned stations.
Note: Since publication two major acquisitions have occurred: *Disney acquired Capital Cities/ABC; **Westinghouse acquired CBS.

It should be no surprise to find Capital Cities/ABC, CBS, NBC and Fox in four of the top five positions. Each network needs a stable base of *owned and operated* stations (referred to as O&Os) to provide a strong audience for each network schedule. Network O&Os regularly clear the entire network schedule, giving each network a minimum reach of 20–25 percent of the national audience (Litman, 1978 and 1993). The new UPN also has a strong base of owned and operated stations to serve as its foundation. Note that Time Warner is not presently an owner of any local television stations, leading some analysts to question the viability of the proposed "sixth" network. Because of this limitation, Time Warner has been mentioned frequently as a potential buyer of NBC, at least of the NBC-owned television stations (Fabrikant, 1994).

Groups that have a strong presence in other media industries are also among the top owners of television stations. Tribune Broadcasting is part of the Tribune Company, owner of the *Chicago Tribune* and other newspapers, a television production unit, and the Chicago Cubs and the Chicago Bulls professional sports franchises. Gannett is the largest owner of daily newspapers in the United States, and also owns radio stations, as do Cox and Tribune. Scripps-Howard, Post-Newsweek, Hearst, A. H. Belo, Pulitzer and Providence Journal also have significant interests in newspaper publishing.

Market Structure

The market structure of the television industry resembles an oligopoly at both the local and national levels. Recall that in an oligopoly, there is more than one seller of a product, and the products offered may be either homogeneous or differentiated. For the most part, the networks produce homogeneous products in that they each provide similar types of programming (e.g., situation comedies, dramas, reality programs, news, sports, etc.) and hours of service to affiliates.

Scholars have examined trends in prime-time programming over several decades. In general, these studies found a decline in the number and types of program categories offered by the networks, a direct indication of oligopolistic behavior (Albarran et al., 1991; Dominick and Pearce, 1976; Wakshlag and Adams, 1985).

Litman (1993) observes that the networks engage in several areas of cooperative behavior (or conduct) as an oligopoly. Litman claims that advertising inventory and prices, compensation agreements for affiliates and license fees for programming acquired from production companies reflect areas of conduct agreement among the networks, whereas television ratings, promotional activities and program quality represent areas that differentiate each network's products from one another.

The network oligopolistic structure is further strengthened by vertical integration—the control of various aspects of production, distribution and exhibition. The networks are all involved in the production of television programming. The number of hours of program production by the networks will further increase once the financial syndication interest rules have been eliminated (Jensen, 1994).

The presence of cable and other forms of video programming (VCR rentals, pay-per-view, etc.) complicates clearly defining the type of market structure. Because the number of competitors are few at both the local and national levels and market shares tend to be divided among the leaders, the television industry reflects an oligopolistic structure.

The similarity of television programming genres indicates high cross-elasticity of demand in the television industry. Studies have found cross-elasticity of demand between the broadcast television industry and the cable industry (e.g., Noll, Peck and McGowan, 1973; Owen, Beebe and Manning, 1974; Park, 1970).

Market Concentration

Market concentration measures in the television industry have primarily been utilized in local television markets. As Bates (1993) suggests, clear definitions are needed in order to measure market concentration in the television industry precisely. Bates used different market definitions for both audiences and advertising in determining concentration in local television markets, and found that over time concentration levels declined slowly, due to the presence of new stations and cable television.

Concentration is more evident at the network or national level, particularly in the form of barriers to entry for new competitors. Litman (1993) points out that economies of scale form a major barrier in networking, as a competitor must reach approximately 70 percent of the national audience to be effective in the market for national advertising. Existing network affiliation agreements currently bind over 70 percent of all television stations (Carroll and Davis, 1993). Further, the investment capital needed to begin a network operation is considerable, involving overhead, distribution costs (usually through satellites) and license fees for programming.

Demand for television stations. Historically, television stations have brought good returns for owners and investors, although a sluggish economy has limited potential in the early 1990s. Studies assessing the value of a television station have found that market size, audience circulation, network affiliation and VHF status increased the economic value of a television station (see Blau, Johnson and Ksobeich, 1976; Cherington, Hirsch and Brandwein, 1971; Levin, 1980). Bates (1988) studied the impact of federal deregulation on television transactions and found the policies had little impact on the price paid for stations. Table 6-4 summarizes television station transactions from 1990 to 1993. As the table illustrates, TV sales improved significantly over previous years, with the average price of a station climbing to $17.1 million in 1993.

The high cost to purchase television stations and the lack of open channels for new stations constitute significant barriers to entry for new competitors in the television industry. Pending government regulation in the form of increased ownership limits could further impact concentration of ownership and stifle entry of new competitors into the industry.

Table 6-4. Television station transactions

Year	Number of Transactions	Average Station Price (in millions)
1990	75	$ 9.29
1991	38	7.19
1992	41	3.02
1993	101	17.1
1994*	89	31.6

*1994 sales of television stations are estimated, although the exact number of stations sold and approved by the Federal Communications Commission was not available at the time of publication.

Government Regulation

The networks and local broadcasters have lobbied Congress and the FCC in recent years to "level the playing field" between the broadcast and cable industries and, for the most part, have found success. One significant action to date has been the relaxation of the financial interest and syndication rules (Jensen, 1994). Allowing the networks to again have a financial interest in the programming they feature on their prime-time schedule, as well as the opportunity to produce and syndicate their own programs, will significantly aid each network's bottom line. The FCC also eliminated the Prime Time Access Rule (PTAR), effective August 1996.

The Cable Television Consumer Protection and Competition Act of 1992 (1992 Cable Act) gave broadcasters the right to negotiate with cable operators for carriage of their signals. Broadcasters could demand that the cable operators carry their station (a form of "must carry"), or could require cable operators to compensate the broadcaster in some way for carriage of their signal (referred to as retransmission consent). Many stations opted for the must-carry provision in order to have access to cable households, but some stations were able to negotiate successfully either cash compensation from cable operators or the opportunity to program an additional channel on cable systems. ABC, NBC and Fox used the latter tactic to gain channel space for three new cable services: ESPN2, America's Talking, and FX2. In other markets, some local stations were able to negotiate a second cable channel to use for local programming.

The Telecommunications Act of 1996 brings further changes to the television industry. Several changes will increase the economic viability of the television industry. The key economic change involves ownership limits. The 12-station numerical cap was eliminated, thus allowing groups to own stations capable of reaching up to 35% of the national audience. Congress has instructed the FCC to look at other changes, including relaxation of the rules for a duopoly that prevent common ownership in the same market. License terms for individual stations have been increased to eight years. Networks can now own cable systems. Existing networks can start new networks, but cannot purchase existing networks.

A controversial part of the new bill was the requirement that all new television sets be equipped with a technology known as the "V-Chip," which will enable parents to block out programs with violent or sexual content. Broadcasters and programmers are threatened by this part of the legislation and fearful of the impact it will have on advertisers. Questions remain as to the constitutionality of the V-Chip technology, which will certainly be challenged in the courts.

Still to come from Congress and the FCC is a decision on a second channel for broadcasters to use for digital broadcasting. Broadcasters want the channel provided free of cost, with a logical time for transition from analog to digital broadcasting (15 years has been mentioned most often as the time frame). Many members of Congress would prefer to have the portion of the spectrum identified for digital broadcasting auctioned to the highest bidders as a way to generate additional government revenues. Spectrum auctions for personal communication services and wireless cable generated millions of dollars in revenues in 1994 and 1995.

Overall, the current trend is toward less governmental regulation in the television industry as regulators work to increase competition across the communication industries. The long-term impact of the Telecommunications Act of 1996 will determine if these efforts will be successful. In the short run, the value of television stations and networks will likely increase as more merger and acquisition activity unfolds.

Technological Forces Affecting Television

Exciting technological innovations permeate the television industry. Leading the drive is digital technology, which greatly enhances the clarity and resolution of television images. Digital technology is the driving force behind the development of an enhanced television system. Presently, the U.S. television system uses a 525-line resolution picture, which was established in 1941 by the National Television Standards Committee, or NTSC (Head, Sterling and Schofield, 1994). Many manufacturers are at work perfecting HDTV (high-definition television) and ATV (advanced television) systems. These enhanced systems will offer better picture quality through increased resolution (up to 1,125 lines), as well as compact disc-quality audio.

Compatibility with existing systems and the economics of converting to an enhanced system are the major obstacles toward adoption of a digital-based system. The FCC has stressed that the new systems must be compatible with the existing 525-line system. Different standards may be adopted for transmission and production protocols (Head, Sterling and Schofield, 1994). The costs for television stations to convert to an enhanced system are considerable; estimates range from a low end of a few million dollars to a high of twenty-five million per station for conversion.

Digital technology, coupled with the advances in new delivery systems available with fiber optics, is creating new markets for interactive television programming and video services. Several broadcasters are already involved in creating interactive programming in conjunction with information services such as CompuServe and America Online (Online with Steve Case, 1994). For example, Capital Cities/ABC is working with NTN Communications to develop interactive games in conjunction with ABC sports, daytime, news and other programs (Berniker, 1994). The potential for numerous interactive applications, ranging from consumer reference to education to home shopping and banking, offers another source of revenue to television broadcasters.

The Economic Future of Television

Although the television industry will face continuing competition for audiences and advertisers through the end of the century, there is no indication that the industry is in decline. Prime-time viewing levels appear to have stabilized as cable and the VCR have reached maturity. In the 1993–94 television season, the combined audience shares for ABC, CBS and NBC increased for the first time in 16 years, climbing to 61 percent of the national audience (Foisie, 1994). The addition of Fox adds another 11 percent, giving the four networks a total of 72 percent of the prime-time audience.

Advertising in the television industry is healthy, with all segments of the industry showing positive growth. Network advertising remains strong, capturing over ten billion dollars a year. Individual station groups predicted double-digit growth rates in local and spot advertising through much of 1994, the first time in a decade that ad revenues were expected to post gains this high (McClellan, 1994). Stable audience shares will enable the industry to maintain strong advertising support.

Relaxation of the financial syndication interest rules and retransmission consent has strengthened the position of the networks and local stations to compete effectively with the cable industry. The elimination of PTAR, as well as an increase in ownership limits, increases the economic viability of the television industry. New technology may open further lines of revenue for networks and local stations. In short, the television industry is well positioned to maintain a dominant role in the electronic media for several years to come.

Summary

The television industry continues to hold a powerful position among mass media industries. The television industry is led by four networks (ABC, CBS, NBC and Fox) who operate in an oligopoly structure in conjunction with their owned and operated stations and their individual network affiliates. Each company is actively engaged in vertical integration and economies of scale within their respective networking operations.

The television industry functions in both national and local markets for audiences and advertisers. Consumer demand for television remains strong, although prime-time viewing shares have been hurt by competition from cable and the VCR, which represent close substitutes for television programming. Advertising demand is also strong in both markets, accounting for a total of nearly $26 billion in 1994. Demand for stations has also grown during the 1990s, with station prices averaging over $17 million.

Regulatory actions limited network power and local concentration during the 1970s. A change in the ownership rules in 1985 touched off a frenzy of station transactions, increasing concentration in the industry. Regulatory actions in the 1990s have favored television from an economic standpoint, highlighted by the removal of the financial syndication interest rules in 1995 and the 1992 Cable Act, which allowed local stations to negotiate with cable systems for carriage of broadcast signals. Recent changes include the removal of PTAR and another increase in ownership limits.

Economically, the television industry is well positioned through the remainder of this decade and into the 21st century. New networks debuted in 1995 in the form of UPN and Warner Brothers. These new networks must acquire enough affiliates to generate a national audience in order to compete with the big four networks. Technological advances may offer new areas of revenue growth as broadcasters develop interactive program guides and other audience services in partnership with software suppliers and other companies. Conversion to an enhanced, digital television system will be costly, and remains several years in the future.

Discussion Questions

1. How has the television industry changed over the years? What factors have impacted television's economic development?
2. In what ways does the television industry reflect oligopolistic practices? In what ways does the industry differentiate itself?
3. Explain how networking encourages economies of scale. Next, describe barriers to entry into the television industry.

4. What is meant by the term *vertical integration* as used in the television industry? Explain.
5. How have regulatory decisions negatively impacted the television industry? How have regulatory decisions positively impacted the television industry?

Exercises

1. Analyze the television stations in the market in which you currently live by gathering the following information:
   a. Technical qualities of each station (class, channel assignment, etc.)
   b. Network affiliation (if any)
   c. Market share (by audience ratings)
   d. Advertisers—local only
   e. Programming during access time
2. Review local periodicals for your market for the past five years to determine if any television stations have been sold, the price for each station and who is the new owner. Are any of the owners in your market found in Table 6-3?
3. Assess the relationship between your local television stations and the cable system in regards to the 1992 Cable Act. How many stations opted for must carry? Were any stations in your market successful in negotiating retransmission consent? If so, how was the station compensated?
4. Review local economic data to determine the amount of retail sales and advertising dollars spent in your market during the most recent year. If possible, determine how much money was spent on television for local advertising, and what the individual market shares are for each TV station.

References

Albarran, A. B. (1989). The Federal Communications Commision's multiple ownership rules: Implications for program diversity and the public interest. *Arizona Communication Association Journal* 18:15–24.

Albarran, A. B., Pilcher, A., Steele, D., and Weis, J. (1991). Trends in network prime-time programming, 1983–1990: The emergence of the Fox Network. *Feedback* 32(4):2–5.

Auletta, K. (1991). *Three Blind Mice: How the TV Networks Lost Their Way.* New York: Vintage Press.

Bates, B. J. (1988). The impact of deregulation on television station prices. *Journal of Media Economics* 1:5–22.

Bates, B. J. (1993). Concentration in local television markets. *Journal of Media Economics* 6:3–22.

Berniker, M. (1994). ABC signs NTN to create interactive services. *Broadcasting & Cable*, October 24, p. 30.

Blau, R. T., Johnson, R. C., and Ksobeich, K. J. (1976). Determinants of TV station economic value. *Journal of Broadcasting* 20;197–207.

Broadcasting and Cable Yearbook (1994). New Providence, NJ: R. R. Bowker.

By the numbers (1994). *Broadcasting & Cable*, October 3, p. 60.

Carroll, R. L. and Davis, D. M. (1993). *Electronic Media Programming: Strategies and Decision Making.* New York: McGraw-Hill.

Cherington, P. W., Hirsch, L. V., and Brandwein, R. (1971). *Television Station Ownership: A Case Study of Federal Agency Regulation.* New York: Hastings House.

Dominick, J. R. and Pearce, M. C. (1976). Trends in network prime-time programming, 1953–1974. *Journal of Communication*, 26(1):70–80.

Fabrikant, G. (1994). Media giants said to be negotiating for TV networks. *The New York Times*, September 1, pp. C1, C16.

Foisie, G. (1994). Big three rebound, gain in share. *Broadcasting & Cable*, April 15, pp. 14–15.

Goldman, K. (1994). "Upfront" ads for TV likely to set record. *The Wall Street Journal*, June 17, pp. B1, B5.

Head, S. W., Sterling, C. H., and Schofield, L. B. (1994). *Broadcasting in America: A Survey of Electronic Media*, 7th ed. Boston: Houghton Mifflin Company.

Jensen, E. (1994). Entertaining talks: Major TV networks dinosaurs no more, tune in to new deals. *The Wall Street Journal*, March 17, pp. A1, A6.

Jensen, E. and Carnevale, M. L. (1994). Fox proves it's ready to play in the big leagues. *The Wall Street Journal*, May 25, pp. B1, B4.

Jessell, H. A. (1994). Quello wants to raise TV ownership limits. *Broadcasting & Cable*, October 3, p. 18.

Levin, H. J. (1980). *Fact and Fancy in Television Regulation: An Economic Study of Television Alternatives.* New York: Russell Sage.

Litman, B. R. (1978). Is network ownership in the public interest? *Journal of Communication* 28(2):51–59.

Litman, B. R. (1993). Role of TV networks. In: Alexander, A., Owers, J., and Carveth, R. (eds). *Media Economics: Theory and Practice.* New York: Lawrence Erlbaum Associates, pp. 225–244.

McClellan, S. (1994). Station-group revenue on comeback course. *Broadcasting & Cable*, April 25, pp. 18–20.

McClellan, S. (1995). Capcities/ABC tops the TV groups. *Broadcasting & Cable,* July 10, pp. 8–9.

Nielsen Media Research (1993–94). *Nielsen Report on Television.* Northbrook, IL: Nielsen Media Research.

Nielsen Media Research (1994). *Nielsen Television Information.* Northbrook, IL: Nielsen Media Research.

Noll, R., Peck, M., and McGowan, J. (1973). *Economic Aspects of Television Regulation.* Washington: The Brookings Institute.

Online with Steve Case. (1994). *Broadcasting & Cable*, October 25, pp. 33–36.

Owen, B. M., Beebe, J. H., and Manning, W. G. (1974). *Television Economics.* Lexington, MA: D. C. Heath.

Park, R. E. (1971). Television station performance and revenues. *Educational Broadcasting Review* 5:43–49.

Stern, C. (1994). Broadcasters split over mandates. *Broadcasting & Cable*, July 25, p. 70.

Wakshlag, J. J. and Adams, W. J. (1985). Trends in program variety and the prime time access rule. *Journal of Broadcasting and Electronic Media* 29:23–34.

Veronis, Suhler and Associates. (1994). *Communications Industry Forecast.* New York: Veronis, Suhler and Associates.

7

THE CABLE TELEVISION INDUSTRY

In this chapter you will:

- Identify the major players, market structure and economic characteristics of the cable television industry.

- Understand how cable operators and programmers engage in economies of scale and vertical integration.

- Recognize the different types of demand in the cable industry.

- Recognize how regulatory decisions have impacted cable economics.

- Understand how technology is increasing the number of channels in the cable television industry.

Cable television emerged in the United States in the 1940s, originally begun as a retransmission service of existing broadcast signals to households in rural areas that could not receive television signals with conventional antennas. These early systems were crude by today's standards, often saddled with poor technical quality, and limited to a few broadcast channels. Cable grew very slowly until the 1970s, when satellite technology created a supply of new programming services in the form of basic cable networks, premium cable services and "superstations."

The cable industry is now present in over 62.5 percent of all television households as a strong competitor to broadcast television for audiences, advertisers and programming. As an industry, cable television consists of many different components, which draw revenues across several different markets.

At the national level, powerful cable operators such as Tele-Communications, Inc. (TCI), Time Warner and Cablevision dominate the cable industry.

Known as *multiple system operators* (MSOs), these companies provide different packages or *tiers* of programming to subscribers, along with the rental of converter boxes and remote control devices. The MSOs have enjoyed a monopoly position in local markets for several years, but a combination of regulatory decisions and technological advances is opening the marketplace for video programming to new competitors. The most ambitious threat to cable's monopoly comes in the form of direct-broadcast satellites (DBS) and telephone companies offering *video dialtone* (VDT) services.

Other competitors to cable include *Satellite Master Antenna Television* (SMATV) and *Multipoint Multichannel Distribution Services* (MMDS). SMATV is a form of private cable, and is restricted to specific areas such as apartment/condominium complexes, motels and hotels. MMDS, also referred to as wireless cable, offers programming packages via microwave transmission. SMATV and MMDS do not involve any franchising through local governments, but MMDS services are licensed through the Federal Communications Commission (FCC). SMATV and MMDS have existed for several years, but their combined market share is minimal compared with the large MSOs such as TCI and Time Warner.

Cable television has operated as a monopoly in most local communities throughout its history (Howard and Carroll, 1993). As cable began to diffuse in the United States, operators were granted a *franchise,* typically awarded on a competitive bid basis by the local franchising authority—usually the local government (see Baldwin and McElvoy, 1991). The franchise gave the winning cable operator the right to offer cable service in a specific geographical area—in most cases on an exclusive basis. The franchising process created a de facto monopoly position for the cable operator, meaning that if a household wanted to subscribe to cable they had but one supplier. In some parts of the United States, *overbuilds* were allowed, meaning an area could be served by more than one cable system. Overbuilds presently exist in less than fifty communities in the United States, although rates in such areas are usually lower than those of communities served by only one operator (Owen and Wildman, 1992).

One reason the cable industry developed slowly was due to successful lobbying by broadcasters to limit competition in local television markets (Owen and Wildman, 1992). For years, the FCC restricted the growth of the cable industry by imposing regulatory barriers that restricted the importation of any programming (referred to as "distant" signals) from outside the local TV market. Eventually, these regulatory barriers were removed, allowing the cable industry to grow.

In 1984, the Cable Communications Act (1984 Cable Act) (Head, Sterling and Schofield, 1994) deregulated many provisions, and also gave cable operators the right to set their own rates for services without approval from the local franchising authority. Cable rates mushroomed between 1986 (when the law took effect) and 1990, outraging members of Congress and their constituents. The 1984 Cable Act also prohibited the broadcast networks from owning cable systems, and limited telephone company ownership to system ownership outside their regions of service. These provisions increased the monopoly power of cable operators.

In 1992, Congress passed the Cable Television Consumer Protection and Competition Act (1992 Cable Act), which included several provisions to limit the unregulated monopoly power of cable operators. The most significant aspect of the new law concerned rates for basic service, with the FCC required to establish new rate structures for the industry. Existing rates for basic service were decreased by 10 percent as a result of the 1992 Cable Act; another rate rollback of 7 percent occurred in 1993. Additionally, broadcast stations were given the opportunity to negotiate with cable operators for carriage of their signals (see Chapter 6). The new law also required program providers to sell program services to competitors such as DBS, MMDS, and SMATV operations. The Telecommunications Act of 1996, discussed later in the chapter, will stimulate competition between the cable and television industries.

Today cable television is a mature industry. Although just under two-thirds of the nation's TV households (TVHH) subscribe to cable, the industry has *passed* approximately 97 percent of all TVHH (National Cable Television Association, 1994). In other words, approximately 97 percent of all TVHH have access to cable, but about one-third of these households choose not to subscribe for various reasons (e.g., don't want the service, cost, dissatisfaction with the service). Competition for audiences will intensify in the years ahead as DBS, telephone companies, and other competitors offer programming packages similar to cable. Competition often results in the loss of market share in most industries, so the cable industry is seeking to expand into different markets to develop new revenue streams, such as interactive television and telephone services (Jessell, 1994; Naik, 1994).

The Market for Cable Television

Multiple markets exist in the cable television industry. As with broadcast television, there are separate local and national markets for audiences and advertisers for cable television. The most lucrative revenue market for the cable operator is the basic cable service, which accounts for nearly 57 percent of total industry revenues (National Cable Television Association, 1995). In 1994, premium services accounted for an additional 21 percent of revenues, and advertising, pay-per-view, equipment rental, installation fees and other services accounted for the remaining 22 percent (National Cable Television Association, 1995). The markets for premium cable services and pay-per-view are discussed more fully in Chapter 8.

The number of cable systems operating in the United States has grown rapidly since 1970 (Table 7-1), reflecting a relaxation in regulations limiting cable and an increase in the number of new cable networks (both premium and advertiser-supported). Although other types of program distributors exist in some local communities in the form of DBS, SMATV and MMDS services, the cable operator maintains a dominant share of the market for audiences. The top 20 local cable markets are listed in Table 7-2.

Table 7-1. Growth of cable systems (1970–1995)

Year	Systems
1970	2,490
1975	3,506
1980	4,225
1985	6,600
1990	9,575
1991	10,704
1992	11,035
1993	11,108
1994	11,214
1995	11,351

Source: Adapted from National Cable Television Association (1995).

Table 7-2. Top 20 cable systems (ranked by number of subscribers)

System Location	System Operator	Basic Subscribers	Rank
New York, NY	Time Warner	1,007,036	1
Long Island, NY	Cablevision Systems	610,717	2
Orlando, FL	Time Warner	492,684	3
Puget Sound, WA	Viacom	424,500	4
Phoenix, AZ	Times Mirror	372,201	5
Tampa/St. Petersburg, FL	Paragon	327,954	6
San Diego, CA	Cox Cable	326,525	7
The Bronx/Brooklyn, NY	Cablevision Systems	197,739	8
Los Angeles, CA	Continental	279,672	9
San Antonio, TX	KBLCOM	260,700	10
Houston, TX	Time Warner	248,390	11
Union, NJ	Comcast	242,118	12
Denver, CO/suburbs	TCI	240,000	13
Honolulu, HI	Time Warner	239,573	14
Chicago, IL/suburbs	Continental	223,334	15
Sacramento, CA	Scripps Howard	213,700	16
Fairfax, VA	Media General	206,228	17
Las Vegas, NV	Prime Cable	205,461	18
Oakland, NJ	TCI	201,220	19
Chicago, IL	TCI	200,922	20

Source: Adapted from National Cable Television Association (1995).

Consumer demand for cable television. Audiences have exhibited strong demand for cable television programming. Table 7-1 charts the growth of basic cable subscribers for selected years from 1970 to 1994. Subscriber demand quadrupled from 1970 to 1980, then doubled by 1985. By 1990, subscriber levels began to flatten, indicating that the cable industry was approaching maturity.

Several early studies found cross-elasticity of demand between cable and broadcast television (Comanor and Mitchell, 1970; Park, 1971; Noll, Peck and McGowan, 1973). Later, Ducey, Krugman and Eckrich (1983) found differences in demand for basic and pay services. A similar study by Bloch and Wirth (1984) found consumer demand was impacted by demographics, price and quality of the programming. Childers and Krugman (1987) and Albarran and Dimmick (1993) examined competition between cable, pay-per-view, VCR rentals and broadcast television, indicating high cross-elasticity of demand for these services. Studies by Crandall (reported in Owen and Wildman, 1992) and Umphrey (1991) indicate that demand for basic cable is relatively elastic.

Demand for cable advertising. Advertising on cable television continues to grow at both the national and local levels, as can be seen in Table 7-3. There are two significant trends in the data presented in Table 7-3. First, advertising on various cable networks (e.g., MTV, ESPN, Lifetime) continues to attract annual increases in national advertising dollars, usually at the expense of the broadcast networks. Veronis, Suhler and Associates (1994) projects national cable advertising will grow at an annual compounded rate of 11.9 percent through 1998.

Table 7-3. Cable advertising revenue (millions of dollars)

Year	Local/Spot Revenue	Cable Networks	Regional Revenue	Total Revenue
1980	$ 8	$ 50	$ 0	$ 58
1981	17	105	2	124
1982	32	195	3	230
1983	60	331	5	396
1984	99	487	9	595
1985	167	634	14	815
1986	195	748	22	965
1987	268	891	33	1,192
1988	374	1,135	52	1,561
1989	496	1,461	74	2,031
1990	634	1,802	103	2,539
1991	710	2,046	118	2,874
1992	872	2,339	141	3,352
1993	1,064	2,669	162	3,895
1994	1,256	2,990	185	4,431

Source: Adapted from Cable Advertising Bureau (1994) and other sources compiled by the author.

Second, local cable advertising, which topped one billion dollars for the first time in 1993, has also exhibited steady growth. At the local level, cable systems compete directly with other local media outlets (e.g., newspapers, radio and television stations) for advertising revenue.

Many cable systems offer advertisers a unique marketing approach through the use of *interconnects*. According to the Cable Advertising Bureau (CAB), an interconnect exists where two or more operators join together to distribute advertising simultaneously over their respective systems. Interconnects increase advertiser effectiveness by offering the efficiency of a multiple system buy, and save time in that only one contract must be initiated (Cable Advertising Bureau, 1994). According to the CAB, some 180 different interconnects are in operation in the United States.

One of the more popular forms of local cable advertising is *insertion advertising*. Insertion advertising occurs when national cable networks such as ESPN, MTV and USA offer advertising availabilities to local systems to "insert" local commercials. This enables local clients to advertise on popular cable networks, usually at a rate comparable to that of local radio stations and much cheaper than that of broadcast television. Clients usually purchase insertion advertising for one or more weeks at a time; spots are rotated around various cable networks on a random basis several times a day.

Major Players in Cable Television

Multiple system operators dominate the cable television industry. According to Carroll and Davis (1993), approximately two-thirds of all cable systems are owned by MSOs. The top 10 MSOs are listed in Table 7-4. Tele-Communications, Inc. and Time Warner are the two largest MSOs; together they account for over 26 million cable subscribers in the United States. Changes in the top 10 MSOs are likely. As this text was being prepared for publication, Cox had begun acquisition of the Times Mirror cable systems, Adelphia purchased a majority interest in Tele-Media, and Comcast acquired Maclean Hunter cable systems.

Many smaller cable operators are exiting the industry due to the high costs of maintaining and upgrading their physical plant (Selz, 1993). *Clustering,* the merging of smaller cable systems into larger MSOs in specific regions, has become a common practice in the cable industry, with a number of acquisitions and joint ventures by larger operators. The major MSOs are able to utilize economies of scale more effectively than smaller operators to lower average costs (On cable's shifting balance, 1994). Economies of scale also enable large operators to negotiate lower prices for software (programming) and hardware (equipment). Efficiencies in marketing and advertising are another advantage

Table 7-4. Top 10 multiple system operators (ranked by number of subscribers in millions)

Multiple System	Basic Subscribers	Rank
Tele-Communications, Inc.	14.7	1
Time Warner Cable	11.5	2
Continental Cablevision, Inc.	4.0	3
Comcast Corporation	3.4	4
Cox Cable Communications	3.2	5
Cablevision Systems Corp.	2.6	6
Adelphia Communications	1.6	7
Jones Intercable, Inc.	1.3	8
Falcon Cable TV	1.1	9
Sammons Communications, Inc.	1.1	10

Source: Brown (1995). Data include all cable transactions through February 1995.

for larger operators. Another advantage for clustering is to generate larger numbers of potential subscribers for the anticipated telephony (telephone) services expected to be offered by cable television systems in the near future. Clustering of systems will allow cable operators to market cable and telephone services jointly to a larger base of subscribers.

In addition to ownership of cable systems, many MSOs practice vertical integration with ownership interests in various cable networks (see Eastman, 1993). For example, TCI owns part of several program services including The Discovery Channel, The Family Channel, Turner Broadcasting System (TBS, TNT, CNN, etc.), QVC, American Movie Classics and BET. Time Warner has partial ownership of the Turner-based services, BET and E!, and Viacom owns or has interests in MTV/VH1, Nickelodeon, USA/Sci-Fi and Lifetime. Other MSOs engaged in full or partial ownership of program services include Comcast [QVC, E!, Cablevision Systems (AMC), Cox (Discovery, E!) and Newhouse (Discovery, E!)]. The top 20 national cable networks (by number of subscribers) are listed in Table 7-5.

Many other companies involved in the electronic media have ownership interests in cable programming, including but not limited to Capital Cities/ABC (ESPN, ESPN2), General Electric (CNBC, America's Talking), Fox (FX) and Turner Broadcasting (TBS, TNT, CNN, CNN Headline News, Cartoon Network). These companies offer their programming to cable systems in return for a monthly fee per subscriber and, like the broadcast networks, sell access to these audiences to national advertisers. At the time of publication, Time Warner was in the process of acquiring Turner Broadcasting Systems.

Table 7-5. Top 20 cable networks (ranked by number of subscribers)

Network	Number of Subscribers	Origination Date	Rank
ESPN	64,900,000	09/79	1
CNN (Cable News Network)	64,700,000	06/80	2
TBS	64,400,000	12/76	3
TNN (The Nashville Network)	63,600,000	03/83	4
USA Network	63,000,000	04/80	5
The Discovery Channel	63,000,000	06/85	6
TNT (Turner Network Television)	63,000,000	10/88	7
C-SPAN	61,700,000	03/79	8
The Family Channel	61,400,000	04/77	9
A&E (Arts & Entertainment)	60,000,000	02/84	10
MTV: Music Television	59,400,000	08/81	11
Lifetime Television	59,000,000	02/84	12
Nickelodeon/Nick at Nite	59,000,000	04/79(07/85)	13
Headline News	56,800,000	01/82	14
The Weather Channel	55,700,000	05/82	15
AMC (American Movie Classics)	54,000,000	10/84	16
CNBC	52,000,000	04/89	17
QVC	50,500,000	11/86	18
VH1 (Video Hits One)	50,200,000	01/85	19
BET (Black Entertainment Television)	40,100,000	01/80	20

Source: Adapted from National Cable Television Association (1995).

Market Structure

Although the cable industry presently retains its monopoly position throughout much of the United States, it is clear that the structure of the market is changing to allow more competitors to enter video distribution. Although not cable systems per se, competitors will offer programming packages that resemble much of the same programming available on cable. The two competitors most likely to attract a large number of existing cable subscribers are DBS services and services offered by local telephone companies.

DBS services. Two national DBS services, DirecTV and United States Satellite Broadcasting (USSB) were launched in 1994 with backing by major corporations, including General Motors, Hubbard Broadcasting, Thomson Consumer Electronics and Hughes Electronics—a division of General Electric (Robichaux, 1994). New subscribers to these services must first invest in the necessary reception hardware to receive the DBS signals; in early 1995 the prices varied from a low of $700 to as much as $1,500 retail. Monthly program packages were initially priced in the $30–65 range (Robichaux, 1994). Two disadvantages to DBS services are the absence of broadcast signals and the lack of interactivity. Another drawback concerns atmospheric interference; bad weather has been known to play havoc with DBS reception. Early sales of the reception hardware suggest consumers are willing to give the new DBS services a try, particularly in areas where cable service has failed to meet the demands of the public (Robichaux, 1994). Other DBS providers are Primestar and Echostar.

Telephone services. The passage of the Telecommunications Act of 1996 allows telephone companies to offer video programming in their own service areas. As a result, the major telephone companies (e.g., Ameritech, BellSouth, SBC, US West, Pacific Telesis, NYNEX, Bell Atlantic) will begin to offer video programming packages that will compete with cable by the end of the century. Telephone companies will eventually bundle telephone and video services together as will cable operators. These efforts will stimulate competition and should lower customer rates for both local phone and cable services.

Market Concentration

The 1992 Cable Act empowered the FCC to address concentration of ownership in the cable television industry. In order to meet this goal, the Commission imposed a cap that limits the number of households passed by any single cable operator to no more than 30 percent. However, larger MSOs (e.g., TCI and Time Warner) successfully challenged the constitutionality of the rule in court, and the 30 percent limit on horizontal concentration was remanded back to the FCC for further study.

Chan-Olmsted and Litman (1988) examined concentration of cable systems and found that the cable industry was slowly moving toward concentration, with many firms increasing dominance in the industry through horizontal and vertical integration. Using the data from Table 7-4, ratios of the top four firms (CR4) and the top eight firms (CR8) were calculated by the author. The CR4 measure was 57 percent and the CR8 measure was 72 percent, indicating that the cable industry is moving toward higher concentration.

Demand for cable systems. Cable systems are normally sold based on some multiple of cash flow (revenues minus expenses plus depreciation, interest and taxes) or as an estimated dollar amount per subscriber. In 1993–94, systems were selling at multiples of 10–12 times cash flow, or around $2,000 per subscriber. Some of the major transactions in the cable industry during 1993–95 are listed in Table 7-6. As clustering of cable systems continue among large operators more transactions are likely.

Table 7-6. Selected cable system transactions, 1993–94

Buyer	Seller	Basic Subs	Price (000)	Price/Sub
Adelphia	Tele-Media (75%)	330,000	$ 85,000	$ 258
Cablevision	Sutton Capital	176,500	463,000	2632
Comcast	Maclean Hunter	550,000	1,270,000	2309
Continental	Providence Journal	750,000	1,400,000	1867
Cox	Times Mirror	1,200,000	2,300,000	1916
SW Bell	Hauser	225,000	650,000	2889
TCI	Liberty Media	925,100	2,513,000	2716
Time Warner	Cablevision Ind.	1,300,000	2,700,000	2076
Time Warner	Houston Industries	1,200,000	2,500,000	2083
US West	Time Warner (25%)	1,149,350	2,725,000	2370

Regulatory Forces Impacting Cable Television

The cable industry has encountered many changes over the years regarding regulatory efforts by the federal government. As Howard and Carroll (1993) explain, cable faced little regulation from the FCC until 1972, when the commission enacted a series of comprehensive rules over the cable industry that aided expansion. Included were requirements for obtaining franchises, limits on franchise periods to no more than 15 years, channel capacity requirements for new systems, must-carry provisions for broadcast stations, the creation of public access channels, and rules against cross-ownership (Federal Communications Commission, 1972).

Most of these rules were later deregulated with the 1984 Cable Act, which sought to free the cable industry from excessive governmental regulation. For cable operators, the most significant aspect of the 1984 Cable Act was the elimination of rate regulations imposed by local governments, freeing the operator to raise rates as desired. Many cable operators took advantage of their monopoly position by increasing rates on an annual basis, creating a hostile relationship between operators and subscribers.

After several attempts to reinstitute rate regulation, Congress enacted the 1992 Cable Act, which required the FCC to regulate rates for basic cable service. As discussed earlier in the chapter, basic rates were rolled back approximately 17 percent, although rates for "expanded" tiers of service, premium channels and pay-per-view services were not affected by the new law. Another provision limited system operators to the number of channels they could carry with which they had an ownership interest (40 percent of available channel capacity). Although not codified into law in the 1992 Cable Act, Congress also required the FCC to establish rules on cable ownership. The FCC tried to adopt a reach cap (30 percent) on the percentage of homes passed by a single operator, but so far any effort to cap cable ownership has not held up in court challenges.

In the fall of 1994, the FCC established a new set of rules for cable operators to add more channels to their basic tiers of service, which were labeled the "going-forward rules" (Brown and Stern, 1994). Under the new guidelines, operators could add up to seven new channels over a three-year period to their basic lineup, or establish the channels as a new tier, in return for up to $1.70 in additional subscriber revenue per month.

The Telecommunications Act of 1996 offers many changes for the cable industry. First, rates for smaller systems (under 50,000 subscribers) will be immediately deregulated if the parent company has revenues under $250 million. For larger systems, extended basic tiers of service will be deregulated in three years. Rates may also be deregulated if a telephone company is providing effective competition to the cable operator in a local market.

As mentioned earlier in the chapter, telephone companies can now offer video packages to consumers, and the new law also allows cable companies to offer telephone services. Industry analysts expect the major MSOs (TCI, Time Warner) to offer local telephone service on most systems within two to three years.

In terms of programming regulation, cable operators must scramble any programming that a subscriber feels may be unsuitable for children. Further, cable operators are given the right to refuse to accept public or leased access programming that operators consider obscene or indecent. The FCC raised the fine for broadcast or cable obscenity to $100,000, so operators will be much more concerned with programming found on public or leased access channels.

Technological Forces Impacting Cable

The combination of fiber optic technology and video compression techniques promises many changes for the cable television industry in the years ahead. Many systems have been upgrading their distribution plant from the old coaxial cable system to a fiber backbone system. In a fiber backbone system, fiber is deployed not to each individual household, but to a *node*, which serves several households simultaneously. Individual households are connected to the fiber system via existing coaxial cable, but at a much lower cost than taking fiber all the way to the home.

Fiber optic cable consists of several strands of a glass-like substance capable of transmitting modulated light via a laser, with a capacity nearly 600 times larger than coaxial cable, enabling hundreds of new channels of information and entertainment to emerge (Head, Sterling and Schofield, 1994). Aside from the fact that fiber is lighter and technically superior to coaxial cable, it also provides interactive capabilities between supplier and subscriber.

One problem with the deployment of fiber is the cost. As an alternative to deploying fiber, cable systems can take advantage of another form of technology, digital video compression, to create more channel capacity. Briefly, video compression allows for the space of an existing channel to be "compressed" to accommodate more channels on a single channel assignment. Video compression has been perfected to date to allow from six to eight compressed channels on a single existing channel. A system with only 50 available channels could use compression techniques to upgrade to over 300 channels!

The addition of fiber optic technology and video compression techniques will enable the cable operator to have more channel space available for new channels and services to offer subscribers in the years ahead. Fiber will allow for interactivity and connectivity between users, a feature not available with the old coaxial systems. The fiber will also offer different types of voice (telephone), data (computer/fax transmissions) and broadband services (television/video), although questions remain as to who will provide this service to the home (existing cable companies, telephone companies, or other competitors) and how quickly it will reach a critical mass of users. A much larger issue concerns how much this new system will cost and how likely it is that consumers will be willing to pay for the new technology and the features it offers.

The Economic Future of Cable

As seen in this chapter, the monopoly structure that characterizes much of the cable industry in the United States is undergoing remarkable change and transition as competitors enter the marketplace for video services to the home. Clearly, the presence of DBS providers, telephone companies, and wireless cable operators poses an economic threat to the existing revenues captured by the cable television industry.

Despite the threat of competition, the cable industry should be able to maintain a dominant share of the market in the years ahead. Existing cable subscribers may be hesitant to jump to an unknown service offered by a DBS company or a telco. Further, advertisers at both the national and local levels remain bullish on cable as part of their marketing mix. National and local advertising on cable is expected to grow at an a rate of 11.9 percent through 1998 (Veronis, Suhler and Associates, 1994).

The development of interactive channels and services, along with the possible entry into telephone services, offers promising new revenue streams for the cable industry. Cable's growth in the years ahead will be more evolutionary than revolutionary, but the industry will continue to be a formidable competitor in the electronic media marketplace.

Summary

Cable television grew rapidly in the 1970s, following the elimination of a series of regulatory barriers and an increase in the number of new services available through satellite technology. By the end of 1994, 62.5 percent of all television households subscribed to basic cable service; cable has passed 97 percent of all TVHH.

The cable industry draws revenues across several different markets including subscriptions to basic and expanded tiers of service, premium channels, pay-per-view services, advertising and converter box/remote control device rentals. Cable operators, represented by large MSOs such as TCI, Time Warner, Comcast and Continental have enjoyed a monopolistic position in most local communities as a result of exclusive franchises. Many of the large MSOs engage in vertical integration through ownership interests of various cable programming services and networks, increasing their economic power.

Today, the monopolistic position of the local cable operator is eroding as competitors in the form of DBS services, telephone companies, SMATV and MMDS offer services similar to basic cable. The 1992 Cable Act reimposed rate regulation on the cable industry for basic services, and took away many of the freedoms embellished in the 1984 Cable Act.

Consumer demand for cable television has been found to be relatively elastic. Demand by advertisers continues to grow at both the local and national levels. Demand for cable systems has also increased due to clustering of cable systems. Clustering has become a common practice as a way to utilize economies of scale to maintain efficiency in cable system operations. Clustering is increasing concentration within the cable industry, with many smaller operators (under one million subscribers) exiting the industry.

Technological forces are creating more channels and more services for the cable operator to offer customers. Fiber optics are replacing coaxial cable, increasing capacity and setting the stage for a variety of interactive channels to allow communication between user and program supplier. Video compression, another way to increase channel capacity, allows as many as six to eight digitized signals to be transmitted in the channel space previously devoted to a single channel.

Although the cable industry faces more competition in the years ahead, the industry will expand into new markets, including telephone services. Cable's dominant position in many local television markets will enable the industry to remain a major player in the competitive communication industries.

Discussion Questions

1. Discuss revenue streams for the cable industry. Which revenue areas are the most lucrative for the cable operator? Why?
2. What factors have led to the cable operator enjoying a monopoly position in most local communities? How is the market structure for cable television likely to change in the years ahead?
3. Why are so many MSOs also involved in the ownership of different cable networks? How is this a form of vertical integration?
4. How have regulatory decisions impacted the cable television industry?
5. How will technology innovations impact the economic development of the cable television system? What will the new technology offer to the operator? To the subscriber?

Exercises

1. Analyze the cable system in the market in which you currently live by collecting the following information:
   a. Technical capacity of the system
   b. Tiers of service and fees (programming)
   c. Number of subscribers
   d. Advertisers—local only
   e. Costs for converters, remote control devices and other accessories.
2. Review the history of cable television in your market. When was the system started? Has the system ever been sold? If so, when and at what price? How has the system been changed or upgraded over the years?
3. Assess the relationship between your cable system and local television stations in regards to the 1992 Cable Act. How many stations opted for must carry? Were any stations in your market successful in negotiating retransmission consent? If so, how was the station compensated by the cable system?
4. Determine if any of the competitors to cable discussed in this chapter (DBS, Telcos, SMATV, MMDS) exist in your market. Try to determine the types of services they offer that are similar to the cable system, as well as those that are different. Why would people choose one system over the other? Compare programming, costs and other features.

References

Albarran, A. B. and Dimmick, J. (1993). Measuring utility in the video entertainment industries: An assessment of competitive superiority. *Journal of Media Economics* 6(2):45–51.

Andrews, E. L. (1994). FCC allows Bell Atlantic to offer cable TV. *The New York Times,*

July 7, pp. C1, C5.

Baldwin, T. F. and McElroy, P. S. (1991). *Cable Communications*, 2nd ed. Englewood Cliffs, NJ: Prentice Hall.

Bloch, H. and Wirth, M. O. (1984). The demand for pay services on cable television. *Information Economics and Policy* 1:311–332.

Brown, R. (1995). Cable clustering makes for active markets. *Broadcasting & Cable*, March 6, pp. 53–54.

Brown, R. and Stern, C. (1994). Cable takes two steps forward. *Broadcasting & Cable*, November 14, pp. 6, 16.

Cable Advertising Bureau (1994). *Cable Television Facts*. New York: Cable Advertising Bureau.

Carroll, R. L. and Davis, D. M. (1993). *Electronic Media Programming: Strategies and Decision Making*. New York: McGraw-Hill.

Chan-Olmsted, S. and Litman, B. R. (1988). Antitrust and horizontal mergers in the cable industry. *Journal of Media Economics* 1:63–74.

Childers, T. and Krugman, D. (1987) The competitive environment of pay per view. *Journal of Broadcasting and Electronic Media* 31(3):335–342.

Comanor, W. S. and Mitchell, B. M. (1970). Cable television and the impact of regulation. *Bell Journal of Economics and Management Science* 2:154–212.

Ducey, R., Krugman, D., and Eckrich, D. (1983). Predicting market segments in the cable industry: The basic and pay subscribers. *Journal of Broadcasting and Electronic Media* 27(2):155–161.

Eastman, S. T. (ed.) (1993). *Broadcast/Cable Programming: Strategies and Practices*, 4th ed. Belmont, CA: Wadsworth Publishing Co.

Federal Communications Commission (1972). *Cable Television Report and Order*, 36 F.C.C.2d 143. Washington, D.C.: Government Printing Office.

Head, S. W., Sterling, C. H., and Schofield, L. B. (1994). *Broadcasting in America: A Survey of Electronic Media*, 7th ed. Boston: Houghton Mifflin Company.

Howard, H. H. and Carroll, S. L. (1993). Economics of the cable industry. In: Alexander, A., Owers, J. and Carveth, R. (eds.). *Media Economics: Theory and Practice*. New York: Lawrence Erlbaum Associates, pp. 245–266.

Jessell, H. A. (1994). Cable ready: The high appeal of interactive services. *Broadcasting & Cable*, May 23, pp. 75–78.

Naik, G. (1994). Hurdle cleared in Rochester, N.Y., plan for wide cable-TV, phone competition. *The Wall Street Journal*, May 18, p. B8.

National Cable Television Association (1995). *Cable Television Developments*. Washington, DC: National Cable Television Association.

Noll, R. G., Peck, M. J., and McGowan, J. J. (1973). *Economic Aspects of Television Regulation*. Washington, DC: Brookings Institute.

On cable's shifting balance of power (1994). *Broadcasting & Cable*, November 14, pp. 38–46.

Owen, B. M. and Wildman, S. (1992). *Video Economics*. Harvard Press.

Park, R. E. (1971). *Prospects for Cable in the 100 Largest Television Markets*. Santa Monica, CA: Rand.

Robichaux, M. (1994). Satellite dishes shrink; cable starts to sweat. *The Wall Street Journal*, October 20, pp. B1, B5.

Selz, M. (1993). Small cable TV operators face an uncertain future. *The Wall Street*

Journal, December 13, p. B2.
Umphrey, D. (1991). Consumer costs: A determinant in upgrading or downgrading of cable services. *Journalism Quarterly* 68:698–708.
Veronis, Suhler and Associates. (1994). *Communications Industry Forecast*. New York: Veronis, Suhler and Associates.

8

PREMIUM CABLE/PAY-PER-VIEW

In this chapter you will:

- Identify the major players, market structure and economic characteristics of the premium cable industry.

- Identify the major players, market structure and economic characteristics of the pay-per-view industry.

- Understand the term *multiplexing* and its importance to the premium cable industry.

- Understand what an addressable converter is, and how this technology impacts the economic potential of the pay-per-view industry.

Premium or "pay" cable channels such as Home Box Office (HBO), Cinemax, Showtime, The Movie Channel (TMC), and The Disney Channel, as well as pay-per-view channels and services, are considered part of the cable television industry because they are packaged and sold to consumers along with basic cable networks. However, both premium cable and pay-per-view are best thought of as separate submarkets, operating in a distinctly different environment than that of cable television networks, which are usually advertiser supported.

As will be seen in this chapter, both premium cable and pay-per-view are important revenue and programming sources for cable systems, but they do differ from the parent cable television industry presented in the previous chapter. In order to understand and clarify these distinctions, we begin with a discussion of the premium cable industry, followed by the pay-per-view industry.

Premium Cable Industry: An Overview

The idea of charging viewers for programming has been part of the television marketplace for several decades. Early efforts were for the most part unsuccessful, and are remembered today by terms such as *subscription television* (STV) and *pay television* (PTV). For many years, the Federal Communications Commission (FCC) imposed strict regulations banning the importation of distant signals into local television markets for fear of competition with broadcast stations. Eventually these policies would be deregulated, opening a new era in cable television.

In 1972, Time, Inc. began a limited, regional programming service known as Home Box Office, which consisted of movies, hockey games and special events, for customers in rural areas of eastern Pennsylvania. The success of HBO led to plans to distribute the service nationally to cable systems via satellite around the country. In 1975, HBO became a national programming service and established itself as the leader of the nascent premium cable industry.

Home Box Office revolutionized cable television. For the first time, viewers could watch an unedited and commercial-free programming schedule. R-rated movies became as easy to watch as a hit program like *Happy Days*. Many households subscribed to cable television as a result of the emergence of HBO, because cable TV offered something unique and qualitatively different from regular broadcast channels. Figure 8-1 charts the growth of premium cable subscriptions and percentage of cable revenues.

In addition to increasing cable subscriptions, cable operators welcomed HBO because the subscription fees became a new source of revenue, which was split between the cable operator and the program distributor. Typically, cable systems receive around 60–70 percent of the monthly fee for each premium channel (Reis, 1993). The average monthly rate for a premium service was $8.80 in 1980; by 1993, the average rate had climbed to $10.48, according to the National Cable Television Association. Total premium cable revenues have averaged just under $5 million a year since 1990.

Home Box Office's success led to other competitors. In 1978, Showtime debuted nationally, followed in later years by several other services. The Movie Channel (formerly known as The Star Channel) debuted in 1979, and would eventually become a sister channel to Showtime. Cinemax began as a sister service to HBO in 1980. The Playboy Channel debuted in 1982, but moved to a pay-per-view service in 1989. The Disney Channel debuted in 1984. Liberty Media's Encore became the most recent entry service to garner at least a million subscribers, beginning in April 1991.

Other services tried to enter the premium market, but eventually moved to the status of a regular cable network. Among these channels were Bravo,

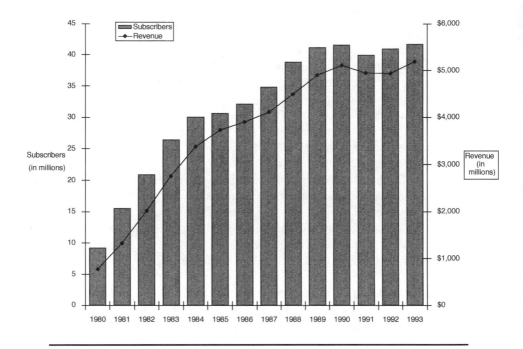

FIGURE 8-1. *Premium subscribers/cable revenue.*

American Movie Classics and Galavision. And a number of other services were forced to cease programming when they were unable to generate enough subscribers to remain in operation. You may recall unsuccessful pay services such as Spotlight, Eros, Festival, Home Theatre Network and Front Row.

Product content. The premium cable industry has had difficulty maintaining subscribers over time for several reasons. Like the cable television industry, *churn* is a problem for the premium cable industry, and operators are constantly marketing their services in different ways to potential new subscribers to minimize the effects of churn. In some areas, churn rates for premium services reach 50 percent a month.

Movies make up the bulk of the programming on the premium channels, but households have many opportunities or *windows* to see a feature film before it appears on a channel such as HBO or Showtime (Owen and Wildman, 1992). Viewers may see the film at a theater, rent a videotape, or watch a movie on pay-per-view. In other words, there are many substitutes for movies on premium channels. In 1991, CBS purchased a package of feature films that included titles such as *Field of Dreams* and *Sea of Love*, which enabled the movies to move directly to network television from the box office, bypassing the premium channels altogether. Although the move helped CBS during its ratings sweeps for the 1991–92 season, the practice has not been widespread.

Because there are numerous substitutes for theatrical movies, premium cable channels have developed different products to attract and maintain subscribers. Among the products developed to date are original movies made for the premium channels (primarily by HBO and Showtime), original series (such as HBO's *Larry Sandler's Show* and *Dream On*), sports programming (e.g., boxing, tennis, and *NFL This Week*), stand-up comedy shows, and concerts. Thus, the market for premium cable channels consists of more than just theatrical film products.

Multiplexing

Subscribers have also questioned the value of premium channels because much of the programming is repeated on a monthly basis. This repeat scheduling strategy is widely used by premium cable programmers as a way to maximize programming resources (Eastman, 1993). In many systems, HBO, Showtime and Cinemax have begun to offer additional channels via *multiplexing,* a technique that results in splitting the programming among two to three channels. For example, HBO subscribers in some areas receive as many as three different channels, instead of a single channel, for one monthly fee. The original HBO channel retains the same schedule nationwide. On multiplexed systems, HBO2 might offer an action-adventure film, while HBO3 might feature an original series or family film.

Premium operators are hopeful that viewers perceive multiplexing as an added value for their subscriptions, which increases the utility of their service (Albarran and Dimmick, 1993). Although multiplexing is a relatively new phenomenon, early studies indicate as many as 7–10 percent new subscribers will emerge as multiplexing becomes available (Robichaux, 1993). Multiplexing will eventually be adopted nationwide in an effort to increase subscriptions to premium cable channels as system capacity expands with the deployment of digital compression techniques.

Program expenses. Programming costs have soared for premium cable operators, particularly for movie packages from major production companies. An expensive trend began in December 1983 when Showtime/TMC purchased an exclusive package of films from Paramount, virtually locking out other premium operators. HBO/Cinemax responded by acquiring rights to other companies, resulting in a bidding war for Hollywood film packages and pay cable companies. The costly practice of program *exclusivity* continues as each service attempts to distinguish its service from other competitors' with a unique package of feature films and other entertainment.

Consumer demand. Audience ratings for the premium cable services have been somewhat inconsistent, reflecting the problems of churn and increasing competition from home video. Table 8-1 reports the viewing shares for premium cable services as compiled by Nielsen Media Research from 1983 to 1994. Audience shares for premium services have declined slowly since 1990, indicating less demand by consumers.

Table 8-1. Viewing shares in pay cable households

Television Season	Share of Audience (%)
1983–84	18
1984–85	18
1985–86	17
1986–87	17
1987–88	18
1988–89	18
1989–90	18
1990–91	17
1991–92	17
1992–93	16
1993–94	15

Source: Adapted from National Cable Television Association (1995).

Consumer demand for cable television has been the subject of several studies. Ducey, Krugman and Eckrich (1983) found differences between the demand for basic cable service and for premium service. Rothe, Harvey and Michael (1983) found that subscribers desired more movies and variety in selecting pay cable channels, and Bloch and Wirth (1984) observed that demand for pay cable was affected by price of the service, demographics and quality of the programming. Later, Murray and White (1987) observed greater demand for pay cable channels in households that owned a VCR. These studies suggest that cross-elasticity of demand exists between basic and expanded cable service, premium channels and VCR usage.

Major Players and Market Structure

The premium cable industry centers around seven services owned by four companies, representing an oligopolistic structure, much like network television. Home Box Office and Cinemax are both owned by Time Warner, Inc. Showtime and TMC are owned by Viacom. The Disney Channel is owned by the Walt Disney Company. Encore and Starz are owned by Liberty Media, a wholly owned subsidiary of Tele-Communications, Inc. Table 8-2 charts the start date, the number of cable systems served, and the current number of subscribers for each of the premium services.

Table 8-2. Premium cable services/number of subscribers

Service	Start Date	Systems	Subscribers
Cinemax	8/80	5,900	7,800,000
Disney Channel	4/83	7,000	12,600,000
Encore	6/91	1,244	5,000,000
Flix	8/92	NA	NA
Home Box Office	12/75	9,300	19,200,000
Movie Channel	12/79	3,250	2,000,000
Showtime	3/78	6,000	9,900,000
Starz	7/94	1,127	1,500,000

Source: Adapted from National Cable Television Association (1995).

Market Concentration

With less than half of all cable households currently subscribing to one or more premium cable channels, one would probably think of the premium cable industry as less concentrated than other media industries; however, this is not the case. The majority of the premium subscriptions are controlled by one of four companies (Time Warner, Viacom, Disney and TCI); hence the market is highly concentrated. Measuring concentration with both the top four ratio (CR4) and the Herfindahl-Hirschman Index (HHI), Atkin (1992) found the premium cable industry highly concentrated prior to the introduction of Encore in 1989 (CR4 = 81 percent; HHI = 2,947); by 1991, the levels had dropped but still remained high (CR4 = 80.3 percent; HHI = 2,297). Data for 1993, compiled by the author, indicate a sharper rise in the level of concentration in the premium cable industry (CR4 = 85 percent; HHI = 2,334).

Because of the high market concentration and the many exclusive contracts in place between premium cable operators and film companies, the premium cable industry poses formidable barriers to entry for those desiring to enter the market. The maturity of the premium cable industry and the number of substitutes available to the audience in the form of regular cable channels, VCR rentals, and pay-per-view also restrict new competitors. Another barrier exists in the high churn rates found across the country.

Two of the newest services, Encore and Flix, do not really compare with HBO, Showtime or the Disney Channel due to the niche they have targeted in the industry. Encore is presently available on TCI-owned systems and, in most areas, is offered to subscribers for a nominal charge ($1–2 per month). Further, the service markets itself as showing hit movies of the '60s, '70s, and '80s, with no new releases. Flix, begun in August 1992 by Viacom, is available to Showtime/TMC customers for a small additional charge, primarily on Viacom-owned cable systems. Flix promotes itself as showing movies "from the sixties to the nineties" (National Cable Television Association, 1995).

Government Regulation

The Cable Television Consumer Protection and Competition Act of 1992 (1992 Cable Act) required premium cable operators to sell their services to other distribution systems, such as direct broadcast satellite (DBS) companies and "wireless" cable services such as multipoint multichannel distribution systems (MMDS). Prior to passage of this act, noncable operators trying to obtain the premium channels were generally denied access, due in large part to the fact that major players such as Time Warner and Viacom owned a number of cable systems and did not want their products made available to other competitors.

The 1992 law did not address rate regulation for premium services; they continue to be established individually by the program providers and cable operators. The government has seemed very unconcerned about the high degree of concentration in the premium cable industry, largely because the programming is an option for the consumers and carries little material that would be deemed important to the public interest. Further, because rates for premium services are elastic, they have not risen as dramatically as the rates for basic cable.

The particular provisions of local franchise agreements between city governments and cable systems may impact placement or the number of premium cable channels available to subscribers, but these regulations are usually minimal. The Playboy Channel, a former premium service, was removed from a number of cable systems after subscribers objected to its content. Along with these complications was the channel's failure to generate enough subscribers. The Playboy Channel revamped its operation and became a pay-per-view service in 1989.

Technological Forces Impacting Premium Cable

Aside from the development of multiplexing techniques discussed earlier in this text, no significant technological developments will likely affect the premium cable industry. Premium cable channels are more likely to be affected by technological advances that allow for expansion of potential competitors to cable audiences—such as *digital video compression* techniques discussed in Chapter 7 and *addressable technology* for the pay-per-view industry, discussed later in this chapter.

The Economic Future of Premium Cable

Premium cable faces an uncertain future. With rising program costs and sluggish subscribership, the services are working on several strategies to attract new and former subscribers to their channels. Among the strategies being implemented are multiplexing of individual services, an increase in original productions by some services (HBO and Showtime), and exclusive contracts with production companies to secure a marketable image and differentiated product.

But will these practices be enough to reverse the slow trend in premium cable subscriptions? Premium cable channels still have appeal to members of the audience who don't frequent movie theaters often and may not enjoy going to video rental stores. Subscription prices need to remain competitive with other forms of video entertainment, and operators need to avoid large increases in monthly rates to maintain a strong level of demand by customers.

Premium cable channels are likely to exist years from now, but revenue and growth expectations are not expected to rise as significantly as they did during the 1980s. Industry analysts estimate the premium cable channels will achieve a modest 4–5 percent growth rate by 1998. Creative packaging, product differentiation among competitors, and successful marketing will be important to maintaining existing subscribers, as well as attracting new subscribers.

An Overview of the Pay-per-View Market

Pay-per-view differs from the market for premium services in the way it distributes its products. Pay-per-view is a form of *event television;* that is, audience members pick and choose among different content choices in the forms of movies, sporting events, and specials, and pay a fee for each event ordered.

Pay-per-view has diffused slowly over the past decade, but the revenue potential for pay-per-view appears very promising. Cable systems use a device called an *addressable converter* to deliver purchased pay-per-view programming to cable households, and the number of addressable cable households has slowly grown each year. At the beginning of 1994, only about one-third of all households were able to receive pay-per-view programming. The cable industry is continually upgrading its physical plant so that most cable households will have the addressable technology in place by the year 2000. Another distribution technology, direct broadcast satellites (DBS), may provide further penetration of pay-per-view services in U.S. television households.

To date, the most popular events on pay-per-view have been programming such as concerts (did you happen to see the Rolling Stones, the Who, or the Judds on pay-per-view?), sporting events (championship boxing and the "Wrestlemania" events have been big hits among the audience), special events (such as Howard Stern's New Year's Eve Party) and movies of all types.

In 1992, NBC and Cablevision formed a joint venture to carry the Barcelona Olympics over three pay-per-view channels to subscribers in the United States. The Olympic "triplecast," as it came to be known, was considered a failure in some respects because of the low participation or *buy rate* from the audience. NBC had hoped to sell 2.5 million pay-per-view Olympic packages; less than 600,000 households actually purchased the package. Nevertheless, many analysts remain bullish over the potential of pay-per-view due to the fact that so many potential customers did not have the addressable technology in place to purchase programming.

Consumer demand. According to data compiled by Veronis, Suhler and Associates in their annual report on the communications industries, the average pay-per-view household buys just under two pay-per-view events each year at a cost of slightly less than $4 per event, compared with renting nearly 50 videos per year at an average cost of $2.30 per rental. Clearly, home video offers a larger selection and a lower price at the present time. But as technological advances enable a household to obtain a wider availability of titles to be delivered with the touch of a telephone or keypad, then pay-per-view may be able to lower prices for individual events and significantly expand its revenue potential.

There are few studies available that examine audience demand for pay-per-view programming. Studies by Childers and Krugman (1987) and Albarran and Dimmick (1993) indicate competition exists between pay-per-view programming, other cable programming, and VCR usage, suggesting cross-elasticities of demand for these services. Clearly, more studies are needed to understand the nature of consumer demand for pay-per-view services.

Major Players and Market Structure

The national market for pay-per-view is dominated by five companies, with potential addressable subscribers totaling over 35 million. The leading pay-per-view services are listed in Table 8-3. Request Television offers five pay-per-view channels (Request-1, Request-2, etc.). Several companies share ownership of Request, including principal owner Reiss Media Enterprises, Fox, TCI and

Wowow. Viewer's Choice, Viewer's Choice: Hot Choice (formerly called VC2) and Continuous Hits 1, 2, 3 are owned by a consortium of 10 different companies. Graff Pay-Per-View owns the Cable Video Store and the adult-movie services Spice and Adam and Eve. Smaller services include Action Pay-per-View, which is based in California, and Playboy TV, an adult-oriented service operated by Playboy Enterprises, Inc. On some systems, Spice and Playboy TV are available as premium services. Because the majority of the potential pay-per-view subscribers are controlled by three companies, pay-per-view represents an oligopolistic market structure at the national level.

Table 8-3. Leading pay-per-view services and potential subscribers

Service	Start Date	Systems	Addressable Subscribers
Action Pay-per-View	9/90	260	7,000,000
Cable Video Store	4/86	185	2,800,000
Playboy TV	12/89	625	9,500,000
Request TV	11/85	828	24,000,000*
Spice	12/89	273	13,000,000*
Viewer's Choice	11/85	540	14,000,000*

Source: Adapted from National Cable Television Association (1995).
*Data reported jointly for all five Request channels, all three Viewer's Choice channels, and both Spice channels.

Pay-per-view is also available in different forms other than the national market. For example, ABC and ESPN offer a slate of college football games on pay-per-view to supplement local television broadcasts. Regional services such as PenVision (which offers Pittsburgh Penguin hockey games) are usually tied to sporting events. Finally, cable systems may provide local pay-per-view channels not affiliated with any national or regional service. These other forms of pay-per-view make up smaller, submarkets of the industry. Although they should be considered part of the pay-per-view industry, our discussion in this chapter will center on the national market for pay-per-view.

Market Concentration

Because a limited number of content providers exist nationally, the market is highly concentrated. Do and Litman (1993) measured concentration in the pay-per-view industry using both the CR4 and HHI indices. Results indicated high, but declining, levels of concentration using both measures. In the study, the CR4 ratio ranged from a high of 96 percent in 1989 to 83 percent in 1992.

The high concentration poses significant barriers to entry for new competitors. In order to establish a pay-per-view service, a new service must arrange for the physical distribution via satellite to cable systems and TVRO (TV receiver only or satellite dish) households around the country and, of course, have a package of differentiated programming the public would be interested in receiving. Both involve considerable startup costs. New pay-per-view services may emerge in the years ahead, but not without a sizeable investment.

The most likely players to enter the pay-per-view marketplace are the major sporting organizations—Major League Baseball, the National Football League (NFL), and the National Basketball Association. Nationally, the NFL has considered offering a pay-per-view package for each NFL team to interested subscribers. For example, if you were a Dallas Cowboys fan living in San Francisco, you could arrange with your cable system to receive every game the Cowboys would play during the regular season for a seasonal charge. The NFL has suggested this approach in addition to its regular package of games available via broadcast and cable channels. The motivation for the NFL teams is obvious: additional television revenues through pay-per-view.

Government Regulation

At present, pay-per-view, like premium cable, is under no governmental regulation beyond requirements for technical transmission. Pay-per-view services were not affected by the changes in rate regulations for the cable industry with the passage of the 1992 Cable Act. However, Congress has shown more than a passive interest in pay-per-view's potential to siphon programming, particularly sports programming, from over-the-air broadcast stations.

In 1991, a Congressional Committee held hearings with the Commissioners of the major sports organizations to determine their plans for using pay-per-view, particularly for mass-appeal events such as the Super Bowl and World Series. The message Congress was sending through the hearings was very clear to the sports organizations and pay-per-view operators: it is in the public interest to have important sporting events on regular television. In short, Congress was saying the public should not have to pay fees by way of pay-per-view for events that are considered in the public interest.

Technological Forces Affecting the Pay-per-View Industry

Earlier in this chapter, the importance of addressable technology was discussed as a key factor in unlocking the economic potential of pay-per-view as a program provider. Another important technological innovation impacting pay-per-view is video compression techniques, which were introduced in Chapter 7.

Video compression techniques allow the cable operator to offer more programming channels to subscribers without increasing or changing the physical plant. Several experiments with video compression are underway in Denver, Colorado; Cerritos, California; and Orlando, Florida. In each case, multiple channels are designated for pay-per-view, unlike most systems, which have only three to four channels dedicated for pay-per-view and routinely program the same material on a continuous basis. No doubt operators hope that the expanded number of channels will increase the value of pay-per-view services to potential subscribers, as well as consumer demand.

Fiber optics have also been touted as another distribution method to bring multiple channels of pay-per-view and other programming to households. Presently, the cable system and the local telephone company are the most likely entities to deploy fiber to the home. Fiber replaces the coaxial cable and offers interactive programming potential. In Queens, New York, a Time Warner system is offering 150 channels to subscribers using a fiber-based system. One-half (75) of the channels are devoted to pay-per-view. In essence, Time Warner has established a *near video-on-demand* (NVOD) system with this experimental franchise. A Queens subscriber can call and order a movie or other event and watch it whenever desired. This system is being observed by operators all over the country, particularly for its profitability.

The Economic Future of Pay-per-View

The economic potential for pay-per-view is promising. Estimates for pay-per-view industry revenue in 1992 were approximately 676 million, despite the poor demand for the Olympic "triplecast" and the lack of significant boxing matches following former champion Mike Tyson's conviction and imprisonment (Standard & Poor's, 1993). Most of the pay-per-view revenue derived from sports ($477 million), followed by movies ($184 million) and concerts ($15 million). Further, when one considers that pay-per-view is not available yet in the majority of the nation's households, it is easy to understand the expectations for pay-per-view.

Pay-per-view providers and cable systems believe pay-per-view will account for most of the revenue growth in cable households in the coming years, in that most households have already made decisions as to the level of cable service and particular premium channels desired. Pay-per-view offers two major advantages to the audience—convenience and exclusive, original programming.

By successfully promoting and marketing these competitive advantages to subscribers and homes that are upgraded with addressable technology, pay-per-view will be effectively positioned to the consumer.

Summary

Both premium cable channels and pay-per-view services provide additional programming and revenue to cable operators, although they are best thought of in an economic context as separate and distinct industries. Major companies involved in the premium cable industry are Time Warner, Viacom and Disney. In the pay-per-view industry the leading companies include Reiss, TCI, and Graff Pay-Per-View.

The premium cable industry reflects an oligopolistic structure, is highly concentrated and poses significant barriers to entry to potential newcomers. Costs for programming have escalated due to exclusive contracts between Hollywood production companies and individual services. Growth projections are low, and the industry faces an uncertain future as it tries to differentiate itself from a growing number of other substitutes.

The pay-per-view industry also reflects an oligopolistic structure, is highly concentrated and poses rather significant financial barriers to new competitors. Pay-per-view's economic potential has been constrained by technology— subscribers must have an addressable converter to receive the programming, and only about one-third of all cable subscribers have the technology in place. Pay-per-view is considered to have a bright economic future as more and more potential adopters will be able to receive expanded types of programming, and as improvements to distribution systems increase the number of pay-per-view channels available to cable subscribers.

Discussion Questions

1. How did premium cable channels impact the growth of cable television in the United States? What sort of economic future does premium cable have today?
2. How does pay-per-view work? What advantages does pay-per-view have over other forms of video entertainment?
3. Discuss the following for both the premium cable and pay-per-view industries: market structure, market concentration and barriers to entry.
4. What is multiplexing? How is it used in the premium cable industry? What advantages does multiplexing offer subscribers?

Exercises

1. Obtain weekly schedules of the premium cable services available in your area, and do the following:
    a. How are the services similar?
    b. How are the services different?
    c. What is the price of each service?
    d. Is multiplexing available for any of the services?
2. Do the same project as number 1, only this time with the pay-per-view channels available in your market. [Omit (d).]
3. Interview someone involved in programming from your local cable system, or arrange for them to speak to your class. Try to find out how important premium cable channels and pay-per-view services are to the cable system in terms of revenues and programming options.
4. Examine corporate annual reports for Time Warner, Viacom, and Disney, and determine the importance of their premium cable operations to their companies. What sort of projections do each of these reports make toward the economic future for premium cable channels?

References

Albarran, A. B. and Dimmick, J. (1993). Measuring utility in the video entertainment industries: An assessment of competitive superiority. *Journal of Media Economics* 6(2):45–51.

Atkin, D. (1992). Programme distribution for pay cable: Antitrust issues in the USA. *Telecommunications Policy,* August, pp. 475–484.

Baldwin, T. F. and McVoy, D. S. (1988). *Cable Communications*, 2nd ed. Englewood Cliffs, NJ: Prentice-Hall.

Bloch, H. and Wirth, M. O. (1984). The demand for pay services on cable television. *Information Economics and Policy* 1:311–332.

Childers, T. and Krugman, D. (1987). The competitive environment of pay per view. *Journal of Broadcasting and Electronic Media* 31(3):335–342.

Do, J. and Litman, B. R. (1994). *An economic analysis of the pay-per-view industry.* Paper presented to the Broadcast Education Association, Las Vegas, NV, March.

Ducey, R., Krugman, D. and Eckrich, D. (1983). Predicting market segments in the cable industry: The basic and pay subscribers. *Journal of Broadcasting and Electronic Media* 27(2):155–161.

Eastman, S. T. (ed.) (1993) *Broadcast/Cable Programming: Strategies and Practices*, 4th ed. Belmont, CA: Wadsworth Publishing Co.

Murray, M. J. and White, S. E. (1987). VCR owners' use of pay cable services. *Journalism Quarterly* 64(1):193–195.

National Cable Television Association (1995). *Cable Television Developments.* Washington, DC: National Cable Television Association.

Owen, B. M. and Wildman, S. (1992). *Video Economics.* Cambridge, MA: Harvard

University Press.

Reis, J. C. (1993). Premium cable programming. In Eastman, S. T. (ed.). *Broadcast/Cable Programming: Strategies and Practices*, 4th ed. Belmont, CA: Wadsworth Publishing Co., pp. 335–363.

Robichaux, M. (1993). Premium cable channels gain viewers with original programs, package deals. *The Wall Street Journal*, March 24, pp. B1, B10.

Rothe, J., Harvey, M., and Michael, G. (1983). The impact of cable television on subscriber and nonsubscriber behavior. *Journal of Advertising Research* 23(4):15–23.

Standard & Poor's (1993). *Standard & Poor's Industry Surveys*. New York: Standard & Poor's.

Veronis, Suhler and Associates (1994). *Communications Industry Forecast*. New York: Veronis, Suhler and Associates.

3

The Film and Recording Industries

9

THE MOTION PICTURE INDUSTRY

In this chapter you will:

- Identify the major players, market structure and economic characteristics of the motion picture industry.

- Understand the different exhibition windows important to motion picture revenues.

- Understand the types of oligopolistic practices used in the motion picture industry.

- Learn how self-regulation is used in the motion picture industry.

- Learn how technology is affecting the motion picture industry.

The motion picture industry in the United States has been a major source of entertainment for decades (Austin, 1989). Movies are produced along a range of genres and capture the attention of audiences across different age groups and cultures. Today, the motion picture industry draws audiences and revenues through several different forms of exhibition—beginning with the box office and continuing through other *windows* such as home video, pay-per-view, premium cable, syndication sales and international distribution.

The leading companies associated with the Hollywood motion picture industry have been in operation for several decades. The early movie companies attempted to establish market power by becoming vertically integrated—controlling all aspects of production, distribution and exhibition, the latter through the ownership of individual theaters. Eventually the government forced the larger studios to divest themselves of either the distribution or exhibition functions through the Paramount antitrust case. The studios wisely retained the lucrative distribution operations in lieu of exhibition (Litman, 1990).

Gomery (1993b) points out that the companies that make up the movie industry have faced numerous challenges over the years, ranging from the introduction of television, cable television and home video to numerous technological, social and demographic changes. The industry has remained stable because the major companies in the movie industry have adopted one of two operational strategies. Some companies are horizontally integrated across different media industries (as in the case of Viacom and Sony) and draw revenues through other areas such as publishing or recordings, which helps subsidize other divisions. Others, such as Time Warner, have adopted a strategy of vertical integration in which a movie produced by Warner Brothers will eventually be seen on Home Box Office (HBO) or Cinemax via Time Warner's cable systems. Cross-promotion is also possible through Time Warner's publishing divisions.

The economics of the motion picture industry, the focus of this chapter, are fascinating to examine. For the most part, the motion picture industry is a healthy media industry, drawing revenues through several important exhibition streams. Industry revenues set new records in 1993 and 1994, following sluggish years in 1991 and 1992 (see Table 9-1). However, the movie business is also very risky. It costs millions of dollars to produce and market a movie and, today, a film is not considered a hit unless box office sales surpass $100 million.

Table 9-1. U.S. box office receipts (millions of dollars)

Year	Total Admissions
1970	$ 1,162
1975	2,115
1980	2,750
1985	3,749
1990	5,021
1991	4,803
1992	4,871
1993	5,150
1994	5,400

Source: Adapted from Monush (1994).

Movie production costs have risen sharply during the past decade (see Table 9-2). In 1983, average production costs per feature film was approximately $11.3 million (Monush, 1994). By 1993, average costs had quadrupled to $44 million; in 1994, the costs jumped nearly 15 percent to an average price of $50.4 million (King, 1995).

The returns on a hit film can be staggering. *Jurassic Park*, a Stephen Spielberg film released through Universal studios, collected $339.5 million in

Table 9-2. Production costs—average U.S. feature film (millions of dollars)

Year	Total Costs
1972	$ 1.89
1976	4.0
1980	8.5
1985	16.78
1990	26.783
1991	26.135
1992	28.858
1993	44.0
1994	50.4

Source: Compiled by author from Monush (1994) and King (1995).

domestic ticket sales in 1993 (King, 1994a). Total revenues from the movie, videos and international distribution will likely reach $1 billion (Vivian, 1995). The Disney studio film *The Santa Clause*, released during the 1994 Christmas season, cost only $18 million to produce, yet returned nearly $105 billion in ticket sales (King, 1994c). In contrast, the movie *Interview with the Vampire*, which featured popular actors Tom Cruise and Brad Pitt, cost $62 million to produce and returned only $96 million in ticket sales. The top grossing movies for 1993 are presented in Table 9-3.

Table 9-3. Top feature films of 1993

Film	Studio	Gross (millions)
Jurassic Park	Universal	$ 339.5
The Fugitive	Warner	179.3
The Firm	Paramount	158.3
Sleepless in Seattle	TriStar	126.6
Mrs. Doubtfire	Fox	111.8
Indecent Proposal	Paramount	105.5
Aladdin	Disney	102.5
In the Line of Fire	Columbia	102.2
Cliffhanger	TriStar	84.0
Free Willy	Warner	77.7

Source: King (1994a).

But the motion picture industry does more than simply produce movies. Hollywood studios are also heavily involved in producing television movies and programming for broadcast networks and stations (Gomery, 1993b). In recent years, several movie studios have merged or integrated operations with major television operations. News Corporation is the parent company of Twentieth

Century Fox and the Fox Broadcasting Company. Time Warner, parent company of Warner Brothers, started the Warner Brothers television network in 1995. Viacom-owned Paramount is tied to another new network, United Paramount Network (UPN). Many industry analysts anticipate the other broadcast networks will merge or enter long-term partnerships with the other major studios such as Disney, Columbia or MCA-owned Universal.

The Market for Motion Pictures

As mentioned earlier in the chapter, the motion picture industry draws revenues from a number of different markets. Our discussion in this chapter centers on four markets: consumer demand for movies as represented by the sale of box office tickets, home video, international distribution and product placement. The revenues derived from the licensing of movies to premium cable and pay-per-view services is also an important revenue stream as discussed in Chapter 8; that information is not repeated in this chapter.

Consumer demand. Demand for box office tickets is influenced by a number of microeconomic and macroeconomic factors. Disposable income, marketing and promotion, demography and competition with other forms of entertainment all can affect consumer demand for filmed entertainment. Box office receipts for selected years are presented in Table 9-1.

Interestingly, consumer ticket sales have kept pace with the rising costs of making movies. In 1993, domestic ticket sales totaled $5.15 billion, improving to $5.4 billion in 1994 (King, 1995). Admission ticket prices have risen steadily. According to Monush (1994), the cost of a movie ticket increased 87.7 percent from 1980 to 1992. Since 1992, ticket prices have remained relatively flat at an average price of $5.05 per ticket.

Annual surveys conducted by the Motion Picture Association of America (MPAA) suggest that movie companies face some long-term problems in holding audiences. According to the most recent MPAA survey, frequent movie-goers, those who go to the theater at least once a month, are attending less frequently (King, 1995). The survey also finds similar trends among other demographic groups, particularly younger viewers. Clearly, the motion picture industry needs to maintain a strong following of younger patrons as older adults (those over 40) attend movies with less frequency.

Home video. The home video market can produce greater revenues than the box office runs, and the majority of the companies that distribute the movies also own the home video distribution rights. The home video industry, manifested in the rental and sale of prerecorded videotapes (and videodiscs), exploded during the 1980s with the rapid diffusion of the VHS videocassette recorder. Videotapes can be purchased and rented in a number of different retail establishments, from chain stores such as Blockbuster to supermarkets and convenience stores.

Home video revenues grew to approximately $14 billion in 1993, and are expected to exceed $18 billion by 1998 (Veronis, Suhler and Associates). Not all sales and rentals of videotapes are feature films, but there is little argument that movies capture the bulk of the revenues in the home video market. On average, rental activity has accounted for approximately 65 percent of revenues, and the sale of video material has captured the remaining dollars. A profile of the U.S. home video market is found in Table 9-4.

Table 9-4. U.S. home video market

Year	U.S. VCR HH* (millions)	% of TVHH* with VCRs	Videocassette Sales Prerecorded (millions)	Videocassette Sales Blank (millions)
1993	71.7	77.0	350	405
1992	70.3	75.6	306	393
1991	67.5	73.3	269	379
1990	65.4	70.2	232	338
1989	62.3	67.6	189	286
1988	56.2	62.2	135	297
1987	45.8	51.7	110	285
1986	32.5	37.2	84	280
1985	23.5	27.3	52	182
1984	15.0	17.6	22	109

Source: Modified from Standard & Poor's (1994).
*VCR HH, VCR households; TVHH, television households.

Home video sales records were shattered with regularity through much of 1993 and 1994. At the time of publication, Disney's *The Lion King* was expected to reach thirty million copies to become the largest selling video of all time. Just a few months before, *Jurassic Park* broke the record set by *Snow White*, which had surpassed *Aladdin*, which had broken the record set for yet another Disney film, *Beauty and the Beast* [Disney's "Aladdin" sets a record for video sales (1993); Sales of "Lion King" video bolster Disney's shares (1995)].

International distribution. The international market is an important part of revenues for the motion picture industry (Storper, 1989). Movies are popular around the world, and one film executive notes why the international market is so rewarding: the U.S. population is roughly 260 million, whereas the rest of world totals around 5.7 billion.

The exportation of filmed entertainment far exceeds the importation of foreign material into this country. According to the *U.S. Industrial Outlook*, statistics compiled by the Commerce Department's Bureau of Economic

Analysis, U.S. receipts (exports) of film and television entertainment in 1992 were $2.5 billion compared with only $90 million in payments (imports) (*U.S. Industrial Outlook,* 1994). In terms of filmed entertainment, the United States holds a strong position in trade.

Hollywood studios frequently enter into distribution rights with companies overseas to share in revenues in the international market. For example, the Fox movie *True Lies* generated about $145 million in domestic ticket sales; international revenues will generate another $115 million, so companies are willing to share revenues with foreign distributors in order to compete in other countries such as South Korea, Brazil, Mexico and Australia (Turner and King, 1994).

There are some problems associated with international marketing of films. The 1991 European Community (EC) directive limits the importation of U.S.-produced films to 50 percent of televised content. Studios are concerned that over time this will result in a significant drop in revenues from European countries if the directive is followed explicitly. Further, international piracy and illegal copying and distribution of filmed material, especially videotapes, is a major problem in many foreign countries. The actual loss attributed to international film and video piracy is difficult to determine, but estimates suggest a value around two billion dollars annually (*U.S. Industrial Outlook,* 1994).

Product placement. Product placement refers to the payments made to movie companies for placing their products in films. It was not due to chance that *E.T.* enjoyed Reese's Pieces or that Tom Cruise drank Pepsi in *Top Gun.* Advertisers paid for the placement of their products on screen. Prices vary; Vivian (1995) suggests placement fees may run anywhere from $25,000 to as much as $350,000. Regardless of the amount, product placement represents yet another source of revenue for motion picture companies.

Related to product placement is the use of advertiser promotional tie-ins with feature films. Again, advertisers pay for the exclusive rights to exhibit their products with movie characters, and are often part of product placement agreements. For example, in the summer of 1995, the following movies were tied to promotional marketing with several advertisers (see Goldman, 1995): *Casper* (Pepsi, Pizza Hut), *Congo* (Taco Bell), *Batman Forever* (McDonald's, Kellogg's, Six Flags, Sears), *Pocahontas* (Chrysler, Nestlé, General Mills, Burger King) and *Mighty Morphin Power Rangers* (McDonald's).

The movie industry has yet to release statistics regarding the amount of revenues obtained from product placement and promotional tie-ins. There is little doubt that the money from these two "new" areas of revenues are helpful in covering the costs associated with producing a feature film.

Major Players in the Motion Picture Industry

The motion picture industry is dominated by seven companies, many of which are engaged in other media industries examined in this text. The leading motion picture studios together control approximately 85 percent of the market. Following is a brief look at each company and its parent owner, if applicable.

- Warner Brothers (Time Warner). One of the first companies in the movie business; produced the first "talking" picture—the *Jazz Singer* in 1926, in cooperation with Western Electric.
- Paramount (Viacom). In one of the largest mergers in American history, Viacom acquired the assets of Paramount Communications in 1994 for $9.7 billion. Paramount is one of the oldest names in the motion picture industry.
- Buena Vista (Walt Disney Company). The Disney studios greatly benefited from the advent of television, and today are a major force in the motion picture industry. Studios that make up the Disney family include Walt Disney Pictures, Touchstone Pictures, Hollywood Pictures and Miramax.
- Universal (MCA/Seagram's). The ownership structure of Universal was in a state of change as this book was in production. In April 1995, the Canadian-based Seagram's announced plans to acquire 80 percent of MCA from its Japanese-based owner Matsushita.
- Twentieth Century Fox (News Corporation). Acquired by Rupert Murdoch in the mid-1980s, the studio became the backbone for the Fox television network, which began operation in 1986.
- Columbia (Sony). Sony acquired Columbia Pictures from Coca-Cola in 1989 for $3.4 billion. Sony has since regretted the transaction, and the Columbia studios will likely be sold (Last action, 1994). Tri-Star Pictures is a Columbia subsidiary.
- MGM (Credit Lyonnais). Another established name in the motion picture industry, MGM (Metro-Goldwyn-Mayer) has suffered economically in recent years. Acquired in 1992 by the French bank Credit Lyonnais, MGM must be sold by May 1997 under U.S. banking laws that approved the transaction (King, 1994b). If MGM docs not turn a profit over the next two years, the studio that made *Wizard of Oz* and *Gone With the Wind* will likely cease operation.

In addition to the seven major companies, a few smaller independent studios also make up the motion picture industry. Orion Pictures is one such company, but several years of losing money has placed the studio's future in limbo. Two smaller companies, Castle Rock (*In the Line of Fire*, *A Few Good Men*) and New Line Cinema (*Teenage Mutant Ninja Turtles* and *A Nightmare on Elm Street*) were acquired by Ted Turner for a combined $600 million in 1993

(Roberts and Sharpe, 1993).

In a highly publicized announcement in October 1994, Director Stephen Spielberg, former Disney executive Jeffrey Katzenberg, and recording industry mogul David Geffen announced plans to start a new studio known as DreamWorks SKG (Turner, 1994a and b). Although the new "dream team" of executives have yet to produce their first film, the new studio has already entered into two lucrative joint ventures for financial backing—one with Capital Cities/ABC (see Block Busters, 1994) and another with Time Warner-owned HBO (Robichaux and King, 1995). It will be interesting to see if the new DreamWorks studio will be able to become another major player in Hollywood, and how long it may take for the new studio to achieve parity.

Market Structure

The motion picture industry represents an oligopolistic structure, with market share divided among the seven leading companies (see Table 9-5). Gomery (1993a,b) explains that the motion picture oligopoly holds a host of advantages that limit the market power (and entry) of newcomers. Gomery argues that the seven major studios engage in cross-subsidization (drawing revenues from other business activities), reciprocity (cooperative behavior), horizontal and vertical integration and price discrimination in establishing fees for various exhibition windows. Gomery adds that acquisitions of MCA/ Universal and Columbia Pictures suggest that the only way to penetrate the powerful Hollywood oligopoly is by buying into the market; barriers to entry are too significant for smaller players to obtain parity with the seven majors.

Table 9-5. Market share of top studios—1994

Studio	Market Share
Disney	18.6%
Warner Brothers	15.9
Paramount	14.2
Universal	13.5
Fox	10.1
TriStar	5.2
Columbia	4.7
MGM	2.5

Source: "Last action" (1994).

Market Concentration

Several studies have examined concentration in the motion picture industry, and all have found the industry to be heavily concentrated, with market power clustered among the top companies regardless of the methods used to measure concentration [e.g., concentration ratios, Herfindahl-Hirschman Index (HHI)]. Litman (1990) reported concentration ratios and HHIs for selected years in his analysis of the motion picture industry. The top four ratio (CR4) measures ranged between 53 percent and 68 percent; the top eight ratio (CR8) measures ranged from 79 percent to 96 percent, and the HHI ranged from a low of 1,100 to a high of 1,600 (Litman, 1990).

Based on 1994 data reported in Table 9-5, the author calculated current financial ratios. The CR4 measured 62.2 percent, and the ratio for the top seven firms totals 85 percent. These ratios are a further indication of the oligopolistic market structure.

Regulatory Forces Impacting Motion Pictures

The motion picture industry has been subjected to both public (governmental) and private (self-actions) scrutiny since its inception. Early governmental regulation and court actions were designed to promote competition in the film industry (see Vivian, 1995). Local and state governments have been known to censor films. Austin (1989) points out that one of the earliest cases of movie censorship involved a 1896 "peep-show" film entitled *Dolorita in the Passion Dance*. This provocative film was removed because it featured bare ankles and suggestive posturing!

Over time, the industry has adopted its own regulatory policing in dealing with issues of morality as a means to avoid state and federal censorship. Today, the self-regulatory efforts of the film industry are manifested in the motion picture codes of the MPAA, well known to domestic movie audiences. The current system features the following rating system: G for general audiences, PG for parental guidance, PG-13 for parental guidance suggested for children under 13 years of age, R for restricted audiences, which means no one under 17 is admitted without an accompanying parent or guardian, and NC-17, which means no children under the age of 17 are admitted (Monush, 1994).

The NC-17 rating has been used infrequently, as the label signifies a major problem in marketing a motion picture. Motion picture producers will often modify film content in order to achieve an R rating, as many theaters will refuse NC-17 movies. Self-regulation remains the primary regulatory influence in the motion picture industry.

Technological Forces Impacting Motion Pictures

There are two types of technological forces that are impacting and influencing the contemporary film industry. The first of these is the expanded use of technology in making films. Computers have changed the way films are made. Dazzling special effects can be created using computers and computing technology. Audiences marvel at the special effects in films such as *E.T.* and the *Star Wars* trilogy, as well as the dinosaurs in *Jurassic Park*. The 1994 hit, *Forrest Gump*, brought a new innovation to filmmaking: the blending of filmed footage with current performers. Tom Hanks (as Forrest) was able to be placed in scenes featuring Presidents Kennedy, Johnson and Nixon, and former Beatle John Lennon.

The second area of technological impact concerns the growth and diffusion of other technologies competing for movie audiences and leisure time. Entertainment systems for the home can now feature wide-screen displays, videodisc playback units with digital pictures, and THX sound systems. The result is a true home theater experience, although costs are relatively high for most households.

Studio executives are also concerned about the siphoning of movie audiences toward other entertainment technologies in the future, such as high-definition television systems, and video-on-demand systems, which will bring high-quality motion pictures directly to the home. With movie audiences declining, the outlook is disturbing. The motion picture industry will need to maintain a strong marketing and promotional position to continue to attract movie audiences to attend the theater as an alternative to competing entertainment technologies.

The Economic Future of Motion Pictures

The motion picture industry has somewhat of a questionable future due to several factors that impact the economics of the industry. On the positive side, the industry is well positioned in that it has the ability to draw revenues across a number of different exhibition windows. These revenue streams are vital to the continuing success and stability of the industry. Second, the industry established new revenue records in 1993 and 1994 after poor performance in the early 1990s. It is too early to determine whether 1995 will be another record-setting year.

Areas of concern for the industry cover several issues. First, will consumer patronage of movies continue to decline? If so, what can the industry do to reverse the trend? Second, what can the industry do to control spiraling costs in making films? With costs escalating an overall 15 percent from 1993 to 1994, the industry must regain control of its cost structures. Third, will international distribution revenues continue to remain strong in spite of the European directive on the amount of imported entertainment programming? Related to this is the concern of international piracy and lost revenues associated with the practice. Finally, how will technology continue to shape and impact the motion picture industry?

Economic forecasts from Veronis, Suhler and Associates (1994) predicted box office ticket sales will only grow at a rate of 2.7 percent through 1998, whereas home video will grow at an annual rate of 7.2 percent. Programming and barter syndication will also grow in the 6 percent range. The *U.S. Industrial Outlook* offers similar projections for box office receipts at 3 percent, and home video growth at 7.5 percent. The two forecasts suggest total industry revenues for the motion picture industry will reach between $35 billion and $37 billion by 1998.

Summary

The motion picture industry participates in several different markets, with the bulk of revenues drawn from different exhibition windows such as the box office, home video, premium cable and pay-per-view, international distribution and syndication. The industry makes a lot of money, but the costs to make and market a successful film costs upward of $50–$75 million or more.

Consumer demand has remained strong, although industry surveys suggest that people are attending movies less frequently, especially for younger patrons. Part of the reduction in movie attendance is tied to the growth of home video sales and rentals, which has grown into a $13 billion business. International distribution, product placement and promotional tie-ins are other important streams of revenue for the movie industry.

Seven companies dominate the movie industry, together accounting for 85 percent of the market. The seven major companies are Warner Brothers, owned by Time Warner; Paramount, owned by Viacom, Buena Vista, a Disney company; Universal, owned by Seagrams and MCA; Twentieth Century Fox, owned by News Corporation; Columbia, owned by Sony; and MGM owned by the French banker Credit Lyonnais. Smaller companies include Orion Pictures, Turner Broadcasting-owned New Line and Castle Rock, and the new DreamWorks SKG started by Stephen Spielberg, Jeffrey Katzenberg and David Geffen.

The motion picture industry is an oligopoly. Although products are differentiated, movie studios engage in similar practices of cross-subsidization, horizontal and vertical integration and price discrimination. The industry is heavily concentrated according to concentration ratios, and poses significant barriers to entry for new competitors.

Most of the regulatory activities in the motion picture industry are internal, coordinated by the MPAA. The public is most familiar with the motion picture rating codes of G, PG, PG-13, R and NC-17. Technological forces are impacting the motion picture industry in several ways. Computers and computing technology are changing the ways that motion pictures are made. New entertainment technologies are competing for the attention and disposable income of movie audiences.

Revenue projections for the movie industry suggest that box office receipts will be sluggish through 1998, averaging only about 2–3 percent growth. Home video and syndication will produce stronger growth estimates for the industry. Total industry revenue is expected to reach between $32 billion and $35 billion by 1998.

Discussion Questions

1. What does the term *windows* mean? How is it used in the motion picture industry?
2. Discuss the different revenue streams for the motion picture industry. Why are box office sales expected to be sluggish?
3. How are product placement and promotional tie-ins used in the film industry? Give examples.
4. What countries hold ownership in Hollywood film studios? Which of the seven leading studios is in danger of closing?
5. What is the MPAA? What are the principal activities of the MPAA as discussed in the chapter?

Exercises

1. Conduct a small-scale survey with other class members of movie patrons. Determine how many times they attend a movie in a month, their age and other demographic characteristics, and other information as warranted. Compare your findings.
2. Review the movie listings in the daily newspaper. How many current films are produced by the seven majors? How many films are produced by independent companies?
3. Schedule an interview with a theater owner or manager. Determine how they decide which films will be shown in their theater, the length of the run and other information. Report on your findings.
4. Conduct a survey of home video rental/purchase activity with other class members, similar to the survey conducted in exercise 1. Share your findings with other class members.

References

Austin, B. A. (1989). *Immediate Seating: A Look at Movie Audiences.* Belmont, CA: Wadsworth Publishing Co.

Block busters (1994). *The Wall Street Journal,* November 29, pp. A1, A14.

Disney's "Aladdin" sets a record for video sales (1993). *The Wall Street Journal,* December 17, p. B2.

Goldman, K. (1995). You will soon see too much of Casper, Pocahontas, Batman. *The Wall Street Journal,* March 6, pp. B1, B8.

Gomery, D. (1993a). Who owns the media? In: Alexander, A., Owers, J., and Carveth, R. (eds.). *Media Economics: Theory and Practice.* New York: Lawrence Erlbaum Associates, pp. 47–70).

Gomery, D. (1993b). The contemporary American movie business. In: Alexander, A., Owers, J., and Carveth, R. (eds.). *Media Economics: Theory and Practice.* New York: Lawrence Erlbaum Associates, pp. 267–281.

King, T. R. (1994a). Box office 1993: Both a record and a letdown. *The Wall Street Journal,* January 4, p. B1, B8.

King, T. R. (1994b). Lion in winter. *The Wall Street Journal,* July 25, pp. A1, A10.

King, T. R. (1994c). Hollywood's blue, blue, blue Christmas. *The Wall Street Journal,* December 19, p. B1.

King, T. R. (1995). Movie costs rose 15%, "a beast" in '94, says Valenti. *The Wall Street Journal,* March 9, p. B9.

"Last action" (1994). *The Wall Street Journal,* November 18, pp. A1, A10.

Litman, B. R. (1990). The motion picture entertainment industry. In: Adams, W. S. (ed.). *The Structure of American Industry,* 8th ed. New York: Macmillan, pp. 183–216.

Monush, B. (ed.) (1994). *The International Motion Picture Almanac.* New York: Quigley Publishing Company.

Robichaux, M. and King, T. R. (1995). DreamWorks, HBO reach big film deal. *The Wall Street Journal,* March 9, pp. B1, B11.

Roberts, J. L. and Sharpe, R. (1993). Turner deal will provide steady flow of feature films. *The Wall Street Journal,* August 23, p. B4.

Sales of "Lion King" video bolster Disney's shares (1995). *The Wall Street Journal,* March 7, p. B10.

Standard & Poor's (1994). *Standard & Poor's Industry Surveys.* New York: Standard & Poor's.

Storper, M. (1989). The transition to flexible specialization in the US film industry: External economics, the division of labour, and the crossing of industrial divides. *Cambridge Journal of Economics* 13:273–305.

Turner, R. (1994a). Three tycoons take on big Hollywood studios. *The Wall Street Journal,* October 13, pp. B1, B10.

Turner, R. (1994b). Three moguls send a message to corporate Hollywood. *The Wall Street Journal,* October 17, p. B4.

Turner, R. and King, T. R. (1994, November 22). Movie makers find that rights to films overseas often pay off. *The Wall Street Journal,* November 22, pp. B1, B6.

U.S. Industrial Outlook (1994). Washington, DC: U.S. Department of Commerce.

Veronis, Suhler and Associates (1994). *Communications Industry Report.* New York: Veronis, Suhler and Associates.

Vivian, J. (1995). *The Media of Mass Communication,* 3rd ed. Needham Heights, MA: Allyn & Bacon.

10

THE RECORDING INDUSTRY

In this chapter you will:

- Identify the major players, market structure and economic characteristics of the recording industry.

- Learn about the historical development of the recording industry.

- Learn about factors influencing consumer demand for recordings.

- Understand the role the Recording Industry Association of America (RIAA) plays in regulating the recording industry.

- Discover new technologies introduced in the recording industry.

The recording industry plays an important role in both the commerce and culture of a society. In this chapter, the focus is on sound recordings in audio and video formats. As a leading source of entertainment, recordings bring pleasure to millions of listeners through a variety of different prerecorded formats such as compact discs and cassettes. As a source of culture, sound recordings have served as a catalyst for change and a reflection of cultural values (Vivian, 1995). The recording industry is one of the most profitable media industries in the world, with a bright economic future. In this chapter, we examine the economic characteristics of this dynamic industry following a brief discussion of the historical development of the recording industry.

The mechanical era. The ability to reproduce sound has captured the imagination of engineers and scientists since the 19th century. Early pioneers, such as the great American inventor Thomas Edison, were only interested in reproducing speech. Edison patented a device in 1877, which he called a phonograph, that was capable of mechanically reproducing sound using a tin foil cylinder. Vivian (1995) explains that although Edison's invention was fascinating for the time, it lacked commercial success because the crude recordings could not be duplicated.

Eventually a wax disc was perfected that could record sound and also play it back. The discs also could be manufactured in quantity and distributed (sold) to different users. A hand-cranked device called the Gramophone appeared around 1887, to be followed years later by the Victrola, which debuted in 1925. The Victrola was manufactured by the Victor recording company, later acquired by RCA and renamed RCA Victor. Today, RCA records still exists in the recording industry.

The electronic era. The electromagnetic or electronic phase for recordings had eliminated the hand-cranked appliances by the early 1930s. Recordings could now be enhanced through electronic components by improving and amplifying the sound. Early recordings operated at a speed of 78 revolutions per minute (RPMs), which became the standard phonograph speed.

Recording technology continued a number of enhancements through the 1940s and '50s. Wax discs were replaced by vinyl, which produced a better quality of sound. The long-playing record, operating at a speed of 33⅓ RPM, eliminated the constant changing of discs associated with the old 78 recordings. Magnetic tape recording was perfected following World War II, and master recordings could be made on tape and then transferred to discs. Single recordings called 45s were introduced in 1949, and became popular with teens because of their low prices. The radio industry embraced the 45-RPM format during the 1950s with the rock 'n' roll revolution.

Stereo sound was perfected by 1961, replacing the old high fidelity or hi-fi system. Stereo recordings were eagerly received by consumers and served as a major force in the development of FM radio. In fact, stereo sound gave FM a distinct identity over AM radio, and led to a gradual shift toward FM dominance (see Chapter 5). Formats for recordings also expanded with the introduction of the eight-track tape and the more popular audio cassette. The tape formats represented a major change for consumers; for the first time, listening to your favorite recordings could now take place away from your stereo set.

The digital era. During the 1970s, digital technology was perfected, leading to the next great wave of change in recording music formats. Using a computer binary code of 1s and 0s, scientists could capture and record individual sound waves in millisecond intervals and play them back in the same way, using laser technology that reads each recorded bit of information (Vivian, 1995). The result was a new format produced on a 4.7-inch platter known as the compact disc, or CD. Compact discs were introduced to consumers in 1983, and today the CD is the primary format for sound recordings, followed by cassettes and vinyl.

Music videos. Music videos were first introduced to U.S. consumers in

1981 with the debut of the Music Television (MTV) cable channel. Although some industry observers feared that the video version of popular recordings would economically harm the recording industry, the opposite occurred. Videos became very popular with younger listeners and also influenced the sale of recorded music. Today, the music video industry has expanded into other formats beyond rock, including country, urban, rap and hip-hop.

Recording industry activities. Recordings are produced and manufactured by major recording companies and their subsidiary labels, and then distributed to the public through retail establishments. The recording industry tracks the number of units (expressed in CDs, cassettes, vinyl and video formats) shipped each year, as well as the total revenues collected from retailers.

The recording industry operates in an interdependent relationship with the radio industry, as well as music video programmers such as MTV, Country Music Television (CMT) and Black Entertainment Television (BET). Radio stations and music video channels use recordings as a form of programming. This national (and international) exposure helps to showcase and promote new recordings and aids in the marketing efforts of the recording companies. Consumers hear recordings on radio stations and watch music videos, which creates demand for the products.

Radio stations and video channels pay royalties to independent licensing firms such as American Society of Composers, Authors, and Publishers (ASCAP), Broadcast Music, Incorporated (BMI) and Society of European Stage Authors and Composers (SESAC) to use the copyrighted products produced by the recording industry. The bulk of the royalties derived from these fees goes to the composers and authors of various recordings, but a small portion is retained by the recording industry firms.

Markets in the Recording Industry

Although other media industries are characterized by a number of different markets in which they offer products and services, the recording industry derives the majority of its revenues from a single market—that of consumers. Most consumer purchases are made at various retail establishments such as chain music stores (e.g., Blockbuster Music, Sam Goody, Musicland, Tracks), general merchandise (e.g., Wal-Mart, Kmart, Target) or independent record shops.

Consumer demand for recordings in recent years has been inelastic. For example, prices of CDs rose about $1 per unit from 1991 to 1993, but were relatively flat in 1993 and 1994. At the same time, the number of units shipped each year continued to increase. Consumer demand for recordings is influenced by a number of microeconomic and macroeconomic factors, including demography, individual discretionary income, promotion, advertising and marketing of new recording products, and radio station/video channel acceptance.

Demand statistics for recordings from 1989 to 1994 are illustrated in Table 10-1. The most striking aspect of the table is the comparison of the year 1989 to 1994. As seen in the table, sales almost doubled from $6.58 billion in 1989 to $12 billion in 1994. Growth rates for this time period were very strong, the exception being 1991 when the U.S. economy suffered a major recession. Nevertheless, the recording industry still achieved a modest 3.9 percent increase in terms of the value of units shipped in 1991.

Table 10-1. Demand for recordings (in millions)

Year	Units Shipped	Value of Shipments
1989	806.7	$ 6,579.4
1990	865.7	7,541.1
1991	801.0	7,834.2
1992	895.5	9,024
1993	1,019.1	10,376.9
1994	1,159.3	12,000

Source: *U.S. Industrial Outlook* (1994).

The year 1994 proved to be very profitable for the recording industry, based on statistics compiled by the RIAA (Record industry in growth spurt, 1995; Trachtenberg, 1995). The 15 percent growth rate from 1993 to 1994 was fueled by a number of popular recordings, including the soundtrack to the Disney movie *The Lion King*, which sold almost five million units. The top-selling recordings of 1994 are listed in Table 10-2. The recording industry is expected to produce growth rates of 10 percent or better through 1998, according to forecasts in the *U.S. Industrial Outlook* (1994).

The bulk of the revenue generated by the recording industry comes from the sale of CDs, cassettes, vinyl and music videos. Estimates suggest that about $7.8 billion come from the domestic market, with another $4.2 billion derived from sales in the international market (*U.S. Industrial Outlook,* 1994). Total worldwide revenues for recordings were estimated at $24.2 billion for 1994; the U.S. revenues makes up about half of this total.

Major Players in the Recording Industry

The recording industry is dominated by six major multidivisional, multi-

Table 10-2. Top selling recordings—1994

Name/Label	Units (millions)	Category
Lion King (Walt Disney)	4.9	Soundtrack
The Sign—Ace of Base (Arista)	4.9	Pop
II—Boyz II Men (Motown)	4.2	Rhythm & Blues
August and Everything After Counting Crows (Geffen)	3.8	Alternative
Dookie—Green Day (Warner Bros.)	3.3	Alternative
Not a Moment Too Soon—Tim McGraw (Curb)	3.2	Country
Purple—Stone Temple Pilots (Atlantic)	3.0	Rock & Roll
Miracles—Kenny G (Arista)	2.9	Jazz
Smash—Offspring (Epitaph)	2.9	Alternative
Music Box—Mariah Carey (Columbia)	2.6	Pop

Source: Trachtenberg (1995).

product companies (Alexander, 1994). These six companies are referred to in the recording industry as the six majors. A list of the companies and some of the individual labels they represent follows.

- Time Warner is the only U.S. company holding a dominant position in the recording industry. Among the Time Warner labels are Warner Brothers, Atlantic, Elektra and numerous smaller labels.
- Sony Corporation, the Japanese electronics firm, entered the recording industry in 1988 with the acquisition of CBS records. Major labels include Columbia records, Epic, Legacy and Tri-Star Music.
- A. G. Bertelsmann, a German company, acquired RCA records in 1988 from General Electric. RCA, Arista records and some thirty smaller labels make up what consumers recognize as the BMG Music Group.
- Philips N. V. is a company based in the Netherlands, and is the owner of London-based PolyGram. Major subsidiaries include Motown, A&M, Mercury and Polygram.
- Electrical and Music Instruments (formally known as Thorn/EMI) of England controls CEMA Distribution, a separate corporation that has several major labels including Capitol, Virgin, the EMI Group and IRS.
- Matsushita, another Japanese company, is the owner of MCA, formerly known as the Music Corporation of America. As this book was going to press, the Seagram Company of Canada announced plans to acquire MCA from Matsushita (Music is the key to Seagram's purchase of MCA, 1995). Major labels include MCA, Decca and Geffen Records.

Each of the six majors produce, manufacture and distribute their own recording products through their major labels and a host of smaller, subsidiary labels. The organization of a typical record company is found in Figure 10-1.

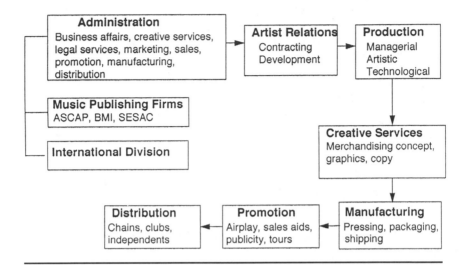

FIGURE 10-1. *Record company organization.*

In addition to the six majors, there are also other suppliers in the recording industry, although together they only account for a small percentage of total industry revenues. These companies include mini-major labels, major-distributed independent labels and true independent labels. Mini-major labels, such as Giant, Chaos and Motown, produce and manufacture recordings, but are not involved in distribution; this is done by one of the major labels. A major-distributed independent primarily signs artists to contracts with majors or mini-majors and is responsible for everything except the actual recording. True independents have no affiliation or connection with majors or mini-majors, and market their products through independent distributors. True independents include Rounder Records, Flying Fish and Cardiac.

Market Structure

The small number of companies that dominates the recording industry clearly suggests an oligopolistic market structure. Alexander (1994) uses two different models of product release behavior to illustrate how the recording industry reflects an oligopolistic structure. The products produced by each of the major labels use the same formats (e.g., CDs, cassettes, music videos, vinyl) and sell for approximately the same price to retailers. The companies also share similar distribution functions (Vogel, 1990). These similar practices are typical in an oligopolistic structure.

Each recording is different from one another, however, which makes the recording industry oligopoly interesting to observe. Individual packaging, promotion and format establish product differentiation. Further, the individual signing of recording artists to exclusive labels further differentiates one company from another in the mind of the consumer.

One noted area of oligopolistic cooperation among the major labels is the recent effort by Time Warner, Sony, EMI and Philips to develop a new channel for music videos (Cox, 1994). A new service would compete directly with MTV and other video channels, pending the successful outcome of a Department of Justice inquiry into possible anticompetitive practices (Trachtenberg and Novack, 1994). Another possible competitor to MTV in the form of a venture between Bertelsmann and Tele-Communications, Inc. (TCI) to start a separate music video channel and home shopping service was later dropped by both parties (Trachtenberg and Robichaux, 1994).

Market Concentration

With six companies dominating revenues in the recording industry, the market is heavily concentrated. It is difficult to determine the actual revenues for each of the six major companies due to several factors. First, only one player (Time Warner) is a publicly owned company based in the United States; the other major companies are all international corporations. Second, individual reporting of company revenues varies; some of the companies report their recording revenues separately, whereas others report recording revenues along with other lines of business. Because of this, concentration ratios are not presented in this chapter.

It is estimated that the six major companies control approximately 94 percent of all revenues in the recording industry (Alexander, 1994; Vivian, 1995). The market share captured by the six majors represents significant barriers to entry for new competitors, in that they control the majority of recording artists, distribution methods and consumer awareness. Over the years, there has been steady consolidation in the music industry as the larger companies have consistently acquired small and medium-size labels.

Regulatory Forces in the Recording Industry

The recording industry encounters regulatory forces in several different areas. The industry attempts self-regulation through the RIAA in an effort to stave off governmental regulation. The RIAA represents the interests of the recording industry as a lobbying force in Congress, and has been successful in gaining copyright and anti-piracy regulation, while fighting off censorship challenges.

Over the years, controversial lyrics of musical recordings have brought about public criticism and calls for governmental intervention. Songs that alluded to drug usage during the 1960s, such as the Doors' "Light My Fire" and Jefferson Airplane's "White Rabbit" were easy targets of watchdog organizations. During the 1980s, the Parents Music Resource Center (PMRC) was formed in Washington, and called for immediate censorship of controversial lyrics, especially those related to sex, drugs and violence (Vivian, 1995). Working within the industry, the RIAA was able to develop self-policing policies in which record companies placed warning labels on controversial material and restricted the sale of some recordings to persons over age 18.

Payola, the practice of influencing the selection and play of certain types of recordings in the radio industry via compensation (in the form of cash or other gifts given by recording companies) is prohibited. Payola represents an example of the interdependent relationship between the recording industry and the radio industry. In an effort to get the produced material aired on radio stations and music video programs, bribes in the form of payola have been offered by recording companies to secure an unfair advantage. Payola is harmful to the programmer and the record industry, and both may be subject to fines by the Federal Communications Commission (FCC) and the Federal Trade Commission (FTC).

Most consumers have made their own home recordings (referred to as home dubbing) from either taping directly off a radio station, or by borrowing a friend's recording and making a copy of it in another format (such as CD to cassette). Anytime recordings are reproduced at home, the record industry loses money, as most consumers will not purchase material that they have already copied. The RIAA estimates between one billion and one and a half billion dollars in revenues are lost as a result of home dubbing. Congress passed a new 1 percent sales tax in 1992 on the sale of all blank recording media (Vivian, 1995). The tax was designed as a way to recapture some of the lost funds attributed to home dubbing, with proceeds from the tax split among the record companies and songwriters.

A final area of regulatory concern regards the impact of audio and video piracy. Unlike home dubbing of a single copy, audio and video piracy refers to the illegal copying and mass duplication of recordings by other companies. Known as bootleg copies, these pirate recordings are often hard to identify, as the packaging often looks similar to the original. In the United States, record companies are protected by copyright laws prohibiting such practices. But in many countries, there are inadequate penalties for piracy and counterfeiting (*U.S. Industrial Outlook,* 1994). The RIAA estimates that the recording industry loses between $1.5 billion and $1.8 billion per year due to piracy.

New Technologies in the Recording Industry

New technologies continue to shape and enhance the recording industry. The latest innovations have centered around new formats for recordings, including digital audio tape (DAT), the compact mini-disc (MD) and the digital compact cassette. Digital audio tape was first introduced in the early 1990s in Japan and other foreign countries. Digital audio tape offers the clarity of the CD but also allows for recording capabilities. Because of the ability of a DAT machine to record an existing compact disc, record companies feared the new technology would harm the industry, especially in the United States. Domestic entry of DAT came about after passage of the Audio Home Recording Act of 1992 (*U.S. Industrial Outlook,* 1994), which provides a payment of royalties to copyright holders based on the sale of DAT hardware (three dollars) and blank DAT media (2 percent).

The mini-disc, a 2½-inch CD capable of holding about 70 minutes of recordings, was developed by Sony. Mini-disc quality is not as high as that of the standard CDs. Philips manufactured the digital compact cassette (DCC) in 1992, which can play both DAT and analog tapes, although the audio range for DAT recordings is more limited.

It is too early to determine how quickly these new formats will be adopted by consumers and distributors. The MD and DCC technologies have been in the market for too short a time to offer accurate predictions. It is interesting to note that two of the companies involved in creating these new hardware formats— Sony and Philips—are both major players in the actual content (software) that these machines will utilize. This is a vivid example of vertical integration at work in the recording industry.

Recording companies are also looking to the Internet as a way to market products to consumers. Time Warner became one of the first companies to offer previews of new recordings over the Internet (Warner to offer preview of new records on line, 1994). Using the audio capability of the World Wide Web, record companies can offer consumers a chance to hear excerpts or complete recordings, although present audio quality is limited. Several artists have released new material over the Internet for fans to download. Although still in its infancy, the use of the Internet will grow as an additional way to reach consumers and market products to potential customers.

The Economic Future of the Recording Industry

The recording industry has shown significant growth in the past few years, and future projections are very stable. The *U.S. Industrial Outlook* (1994) shows expected double digit growth of at least 10 percent for the recording industry through 1998; Veronis, Suhler and Associates (1994) offers a more conservative growth rate of 7.4 percent.

Compact discs and cassettes sell millions of units each year, and CDs will continue to outsell cassettes in the future. New formats such as the mini-disc, DAT and the digital compact disc are expected to develop slowly, but will still contribute to industry growth.

International markets and expansion will also help industry growth. The most successful recording artists in the world are from the United States, and the popularity of domestic recording artists and the wide acceptance of recordings in English will help growth in international markets.

Summary

The recording industry is one of the most profitable media industries in the United States and abroad. It is also an industry marked by technological change and progress, having evolved from a mechanical system to an electromagnetic system to the current system employing digital technology.

Recordings are produced and manufactured by major companies and their subsidiary labels, and then distributed to the public through retail establishments. The recording industry maintains an interdependent relationship with the radio industry. The recording industry supplies needed programming to radio stations, and stations provide much needed exposure to consumers. Music video services also enjoy a similar relationship with the recording industry.

Consumers form the primary market for recordings, which are acquired from chain music stores, retailers and independent record shops. Demand for recordings has remained inelastic through the 1990s; units shipped and revenues continue to rise despite increases in the price of recordings. Revenues for the domestic recording industry reached a record $12 billion in 1994, about half of the world total.

The recording industry is dominated by six major companies: Time Warner, Sony, Bertelsmann, Philips, EMI and Matsushita. The six companies comprise an oligopolistic market structure, and account for over 90 percent of industry revenues. The market is heavily concentrated with significant barriers to entry for new competitors.

The recording industry is primarily self-regulated through the RIAA, its industry association. The RIAA has been successful in securing copyright and anti-piracy regulation, while fighting off censorship challenges from groups such as the PMRC.

New technologies continue to emerge in the recording industry. Recent innovations include digital audio tape systems and media, mini-compact discs, and digital compact cassettes. The Internet will become an important resource in marketing recording industry products to consumers.

The recording industry is expected to grow at a rate estimated at 7–10 percent over the next few years. Strong sales, expansion into international markets and the development of new recording technologies will all aid industry growth.

Discussion Questions

1. How did the three eras of development (mechanical, electronic, digital) change the recording industry?
2. What are the various functions of a record company?
3. The recording industry primarily serves a single market. How does this differ from other media industries examined in this text?
4. What do we mean when we say demand for recordings is inelastic? What factors influence consumer demand for recordings?
5. The recording industry represents an oligopolistic structure. Why is it unlikely that any new competitors will emerge to challenge the six major recording companies?

Exercises

1. Pick out one of the six major labels identified in the text and answer the following:
   a. What are the sublabels under this company?
   b. What recording artists appear on these labels?
   c. What formats (CD, cassette, vinyl) are products released on?
   d. Where (locally) can you find this company's recordings for sale?
   e. Are products licensed under ASCAP, BMI or SESAC?
2. Find a list of top-selling recordings in your area, and compare it with a national listing in a publication such as *Billboard* or *Radio and Records*. What recordings are similar on the list? Which ones are different?
3. Compare the costs for local recordings at several different retail establishments. Are prices lower at one type of location than another? How do local prices compare with prices offered by music clubs such as BMG and Sony?
4. Which current recordings contain controversial lyrics or parental advisory labels? Do these recordings appear on the local top-seller list?

References

Alexander, P. J. (1994). Entry barriers, release behavior, and multi-product firms in the music recording industry. *Review of Industrial Organization* 9:85–98.

Cox, M. (1994). Four record firms plan new channel for music videos. *The Wall Street Journal*, February 1, p. B1.

Music is the key to Seagram's purchase of MCA (1995). *The Dallas Morning News*, April 10, pp. 1D, 4D.

Record industry in growth spurt (1995). *The Dallas Morning News*, February 10, p. 25A.

Standard & Poor's. (1994). *Standard & Poor's Industry Surveys*. New York: Standard & Poor's.

Trachtenberg, J. A. (1995). New artists and older buyers inspire a record year in music. *The Wall Street Journal*, February 16, pp. B1, B10.

Trachtenberg, J. A. and Novack, V. (1994). Five music companies face inquiry into plans to begin video channel in '95. *The Wall Street Journal*, July 25, p. B4.

Trachtenberg, J. A. and Robichaux, M. (1994). TCI and Bertlesmann unit drop plans for music, home-shopping channel. *The Wall Street Journal*, June 6, p. B6.

U.S. Industrial Outlook. (1994). Washington, DC: U.S. Department of Commerce.

Veronis, Suhler and Associates (1994). *Communications Industry Report.* New York: Author.

Vivian, J. (1995). *The Media of Mass Communication,* 3rd ed. Needham Heights, MA: Allyn & Bacon.

Vogel, H. L. (1990). *Entertainment Industry Economics: A Guide for Financial Analysis*, 2nd ed. Cambridge: Cambridge University Press.

Warner to offer preview of new records on line (1994). *The Wall Street Journal*, August 9, p. A3.

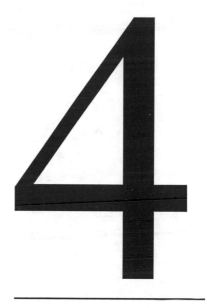

The
Print
Industries

11

THE NEWSPAPER INDUSTRY

In this chapter you will:

- Identify the major players, market structure and economic characteristics of the newspaper industry.

- Understand the three types of advertising found in newspapers.

- Recognize how newspaper chains dominate the industry.

- Learn how economies of scope and barriers to entry have led to single newspapers in many cities.

- Learn about Joint Operating Agreements (JOAs) and their role in the newspaper industry.

The newspaper industry represents one of the oldest forms of mass media in the United States, second only to the book publishing industry. Throughout its colorful history, the newspaper industry has been an important source of social, political and cultural information to generations of readers. The newspaper industry has also played a pivotal role in commerce, serving as a major commercial entity linking advertisers and consumers.

Newspapers offer something for every type of reader. Local, national and international news represent the major categories of newspaper content consumed by most readers. Sports, weather, editorials, advice, columns and features, comics, puzzles and games, advertising and other types of data are among the regular sections found in many metropolitan and hometown newspapers. Unlike other forms of publishing, the daily newspaper is a product that has a life of only 24 hours or less!

Newspapers remain popular as an important source of news and information, even in today's saturated electronic media environment. Statistics from the Newspaper Association of America (NAA) indicate that 61.7 percent of all adults read a daily newspaper on an average weekday, far more than those exposed to a network TV news broadcast (Newspaper Association of America, 1994). The Sunday newspaper has an even higher reach. It is estimated that 69 percent of all adults read a Sunday newspaper during an average week (Newspaper Association of America, 1994).

Newspapers continue to be the most profitable form of mass media in the United States. Newspapers routinely attract the largest percentage of advertising expenditures when compared with television, direct mail and radio, although the margin between newspapers and television has shrunk considerably over the past decade. In 1993, total newspaper advertising revenue (national, retail and classified) was estimated at $31.9 billion (Newspaper Association of America, 1994). Combined with weekly subscriber fees and the sale of papers through newsstands and other outlets, the newspaper industry currently attracts over $40 billion through advertising and circulation sales (Picard, 1993).

In addition to daily and Sunday papers, weekly newspapers (some are called suburban papers) reach an estimated 45 million readers a week (Vivian, 1995). Nationally distributed newspapers, such as *The Wall Street Journal*, *The New York Times* and *USA Today* are regularly read by thousands of readers.

The newspaper industry faces several issues of concern, including a decline in the number of daily newspapers, sluggish circulation, the rising cost of newsprint, and rapidly changing technology. As this chapter illustrates, newspapers are unique from other mass media industries in terms of their characteristics and market structure.

The Market for Newspapers

The newspaper industry is characterized by different markets for both circulation and advertising. Daily newspapers, which consist of morning and evening newspapers and Sunday editions, represent the most visible form of newspaper activity. Weeklies or suburban papers make up a second, smaller market. Each of these circulation markets is discussed below.

Daily newspapers. There are approximately 1,566 daily newspapers in operation in the United States. Picard (1993) reports that 90 percent of these papers exist as the only newspaper in their city of operation. Table 11-1 reports data for morning, evening and Sunday newspapers for selected years between 1946 and 1993. Three trends are obvious when examining the table. First, the total number of daily newspapers has declined over the years, from a high of 1,772 in 1950 to 1,556 reported at the end of 1993. Second, evening papers continue to outnumber morning papers, although the gap separating morning and evening papers has narrowed over the years. Last, the number of Sunday newspapers almost doubled between 1946 and 1992, with a slight decline reported for 1993.

Table 11-1. Number of U.S. daily newspapers

Year	Morning	Evening	Total M&E	Sunday
1946	334	1,429	1,763	497
1950	322	1,450	1,772	549
1955	316	1,454	1,760	541
1960	312	1,459	1,763	563
1965	320	1,444	1,751	562
1970	334	1,429	1,748	586
1975	339	1,436	1,756	639
1980	387	1,388	1,745	735
1985	482	1,220	1,676	798
1986	499	1,188	1,657	802
1987	511	1,166	1,645	820
1988	529	1,141	1,642	840
1989	530	1,125	1,626	847
1990	559	1,084	1,611	863
1991	571	1,042	1,586	874
1992	596	995	1,570	891
1993	621	956	1,556	889

Source: Modified from Newspaper Association of America (1994).

According to the Newspaper Association of America (1994), total annual circulation for morning papers was 43,053,747, the highest figure reported in newspaper history. Annual circulation for evening papers was 16,761,294, a drop of nearly one million papers from 1992. Evening newspaper circulation has fallen steadily since 1965, in conjunction with the decline in the number of evening papers. Sunday circulation has remained relatively flat since 1989. In 1993, Sunday circulation was reported at 62,643,379 papers.

Average daily circulation (ADC) is the best indicator of consumer demand for daily newspapers. The twenty largest daily newspapers are found in Table 11-2. The two largest papers, *The Wall Street Journal* and *USA Today,* are considered national newspapers in the sense that they do not serve a specific geographic area or retail trading zone (RTZ), a term commonly used in the newspaper industry. Other papers on this list are also available in many parts of the country and thus widely read, including *The New York Times, The Washington Post,* and the *Chicago Tribune.* According to Veronis, Suhler and Associates (1994), weekday circulation accounts for approximately 12 percent of all newspaper revenues, and Sunday circulation accounts for 5 percent of total revenues.

Circulation elasticity of demand, or the "circulation spiral" is one factor

*Table 11-2. Largest U.S. dailies by circulation (average daily circula-
tion)*

The Wall Street Journal	1,818,562	(m)
USA Today	1,494,929	(m)
The New York Times	1,141,366	(m)
Los Angeles Times	1,089,690	(m)
The Washington Post	813,908	(m)
Daily News, New York	764,070	(m)
Newsday	747,890	(all day)
Chicago Tribune	690,842	(m)
Detroit Free Press	556,116	(m)
San Francisco Chronicle	544,253	(m)
Chicago Sun-Times	535,793	(m)
The Boston Globe	507,647	(m)
The Dallas Morning News	493,837	(m)
The Philadelphia Inquirer	486,568	(m)
The Star-Ledger, Newark	473,558	(m)
Houston Chronicle	413,448	(all day)
Star Tribune, Minneapolis	410,754	(m)
The Plain Dealer, Cleveland	395,791	(m)
New York Post	394,431	(m)
Miami Herald	386,664	(m)

Source: Modified from Newspaper Association of America (1994).
Note: m = morning edition.

contributing to the decline of daily newspapers (see Gustafsson, 1978). In cities
served by more than one newspaper, one paper will often be the "leader" in
terms of circulation and advertising linage. Advertisers will tend to place more
dollars in the paper that attracts the most readers, thus, the "second" paper in the
market will receive a disproportional lower share of advertising dollars. As the
leader attracts more readers and advertisers over time, the second paper faces a
downward-sloping circulation spiral. Picard (1993) claims that once the leading
paper attracts as much as 55–60 percent of the circulation in a market, serious
financial problems will result for the other paper.

Weekly newspapers. The Newspaper Association of America estimates that
there are 7,437 weekly newspapers with an average circulation of 7,629 across
the United States (Newspaper Association of America, 1994). Total weekly
circulation is estimated at 56 million papers. Data for U.S. weekly newspapers
between 1960 and 1993 are included in Table 11-3.

Weekly newspapers are very popular in both rural and suburban communities where local news and events are emphasized. Large metropolitan cities can
only devote so much space to news in the suburban areas, so weekly papers have
an eager market for readers desiring more local news coverage. Local retail
advertisers find that weekly newspapers are much cheaper than their larger
metropolitan counterparts, and provide greater efficiency in reaching target
audiences.

Table 11-3. U.S. weekly newspapers

Year	Total Weekly Newspapers	Average Circulation	Total Weekly Circulation
1960	8,174	2,566	20,974,338
1965	8,061	3,106	25,036,031
1970	7,612	3,660	27,857,332
1975	7,612	4,715	35,892,409
1980	7,954	5,324	42,347,512
1985	7,704	6,359	48,988,801
1986	7,711	6,497	50,098,000
1987	7,600	6,262	47,593,000
1988	7,498	6,894	51,691,451
1989	7,606	6,958	52,919,846
1990	7,550	7,309	55,181,047
1991	7,476	7,323	54,746,332
1992	7,417	7,358	54,577,034
1993	7,437	7,629	56,734,526

Source: Modified from Newspaper Association of America (1994).

Market for advertising. As reported earlier, newspapers capture the largest percentage of advertising dollars among media industries in the United States. In 1993, newspapers accounted for 23.1 percent of all advertising expenditures (Newspaper Association of America, 1994). In fact, advertising takes up about 50–60 percent of the total space in a daily newspaper; slightly higher on Sundays.

Newspapers draw advertising revenues across three separate areas. National advertising represents the smallest category of revenues and is used primarily by major companies to help market products and services that are distributed nationally. Retail advertising is the most lucrative area for newspapers, and is derived from local businesses in the same RTZ as the newspaper. Classified advertising is used primarily by individuals and small businesses to reach buyers and sellers across different categories (automobiles, appliances, housing, miscellaneous, etc.).

Newspaper advertising revenues for selected years are detailed in Table 11-4. Total newspaper advertising is expected to grow at an average rate of 5.4 percent through 1997, to reach an all-time high of $40 billion (Veronis, Suhler and Associates, 1994).

Major Players in the Newspaper Industry

The majority of the newspapers in the United States are owned by corporations or groups. In the newspaper industry, the term *chain* is used to represent group owned newspapers. The practice of acquiring newspaper chains

*Table 11-4.   U.S. daily newspaper advertising expenditures (millions of
dollars)*

Year	National	Retail	Classified	Total Advertising
1950	$ 518	$ 1,175	$ 377	$ 2,070
1955	712	1,755	610	3,077
1960	778	2,100	803	3,681
1965	783	2,429	1,214	4,426
1970	891	3,292	1,521	5,704
1975	1,109	4,966	2,159	8,234
1980	1,963	8,609	4,222	14,794
1985	3,352	13,443	8,375	25,170
1986	3,376	14,311	9,303	26,990
1987	3,494	15,227	10,691	29,412
1988	3,821	15,790	11,586	31,197
1989	3,948	16,504	11,916	32,368
1990	4,122	16,652	11,506	32,280
1991	3,924	15,839	10,587	30,349
1992	3,834	16,041	10,764	30,639
1993	3,853	16,874	11,179	31,906

Source: Modified from Newspaper Association of America (1994).

began in the 1880s, when larger publishers began acquiring a number of
newspapers (Vivian, 1995).

Over 85 percent of all newspapers are owned by large corporations. The
largest chains are listed in Table 11-5, ranked according to daily circulation
statistics. Chain ownership surged during the 1970s and 1980s, with record
prices paid for many newspapers. A slowdown in the economy during the early
1990s had tremendous impact on the newspaper industry as an investment.
Between 1989 and 1992 the newspaper industry grew at an annual rate of only
1 percent (Veronis, Suhler and Associates, 1994).

Many of the companies found in Table 11-5 are among the most profitable
companies in the world. As observed in earlier chapters, many of these
companies also have significant ownership interests in other areas of the mass
media. Companies with holdings in other media include major publishers
Gannett, Newhouse, Tribune, Cox and Capital Cities/ABC. Foreign ownership
of newspapers has increased rapidly during the past two decades. It is estimated
that 13 percent of all U.S. newspapers are foreign controlled. Thomson
Newspapers, a Canadian company, is the largest single foreign owner with
approximately 109 dailies (Newspaper Association of America, 1994).

Market Structure

The Newspaper Association of America reports that at the beginning of

Table 11-5. Largest U.S. newspaper companies

Company Name	Daily Circulation	Number Dailies
Gannett Co. Inc.	5,843,238	83
Knight-Ridder Inc.	3,678,200	28
Newhouse Newspapers	2,983,429	26
Times Mirror Co.	2,713,742	11
The New York Times Co.	2,471,587	25
Dow Jones & Co. Inc.	2,377,538	22
Thomson Newspapers Inc.	2,072,649	109
Tribune Co.	1,355,630	6
Cox Enterprises Inc.	1,312,239	19
Scripps Howard	1,300,391	19
Hearst Newspapers	1,256,202	12
MediaNews Group	1,045,406	17
Freedom Newspapers Inc.	943,227	26
The Washington Post Co.	865,781	2
Central Newspapers	817,853	9
McClatchy Newspapers	809,578	12
Stephens Group Inc.	750,945	54
Capital Cities/ABC Inc.	744,291	8
Copley Newspapers	738,996	10
The Chronicle Publishing Co.	711,682	4

Source: Modified from Newspaper Association of America (1994).

1994, only 33 cities were served by two or more newspapers operating under separate ownership (Newspaper Association of America, 1994; Figure 3-11). As such, the newspaper industry represents a monopolistic market structure across most of the country.

The cost structures of producing a newspaper have helped to promote a monopolistic structure for newspapers (Picard, 1988b). The "first copy" costs to produce a newspaper include considerable fixed and variable costs. Once the first copy is produced, the publisher is able to lower the actual cost per issue through the mass production and distribution of other copies of the paper. Economies of scale lower the costs as more and more papers are produced (Rosse and Dertouzous, 1979).

For a rather simplistic example, let's assume that it costs a publisher $10,000 to produce a single copy of the newspaper. As succeeding copies of the paper are reproduced, the cost per issue drops rapidly. Producing 1,000 papers lowers the cost per paper to $10; producing 100,000 papers would lower the cost per paper to just 10 cents an issue. No doubt, producing 100,000 papers would also increase some of the variable costs (ink and newsprint) associated with newspaper publishing, but economies of scale are still realized.

Picard (1993) claims that scholars sometimes incorrectly consider newspapers to be natural monopolies. In reality, natural monopolies are able to engage in continuous economies of scale, which is rare in the newspaper industry. Litman (1988) adds that such a situation is only possible where a single firm produces a newspaper in a market, and the firm controls the entire market and exercises significant power.

Market Concentration

Newspaper markets are highly concentrated due to a monopolistic market structure. Picard (1988a) calculated concentration ratios for national and local newspaper markets based on circulation data. He found that although newspaper markets are highly concentrated, concentration increases as the size of the market decreases.

Concentration is a particular concern in the newspaper industry, as newspapers "operate not only in the marketplace for goods and services but also in the marketplace for ideas" (Picard, 1988a, p. 62). The rise in chain ownership, coupled with market concentration, has raised industry concerns about the push for profits at the expense of journalistic endeavors, diversity of expression and balanced presentation. Dertouzous and Trautman (1990) argue that the lack of direct competition in many cities is the result of scale economies in production, advertising, circulation and news.

The concentration of newspaper markets as well as the costs required to start a newspaper pose considerable barriers to entry for new competitors desiring to enter the market. Wirth (1986) has shown that it is easier to enter the market for local broadcasting than to begin a newspaper.

Regulatory Forces Impacting Newspapers

Newspapers are subject to very few regulations at either the local, state or federal levels. In fact, most policies directed toward newspapers have been designed to enhance the economics of the industry. Included are such provisions as exemptions from sales taxes on advertising, and relaxation of wage and hour laws for employees.

No doubt, the most significant legislative reform to impact the newspaper industry was the 1970 Newspaper Preservation Act. Congress passed the act in order to promote a diversity of expression in those communities where the market could no longer support two competing newspapers. The act allows the establishment of JOAs among newspaper firms. Under a JOA, editorial operations remain separate, but all other operations (printing, advertising, distribution, etc.) are combined. According to the NAA, there are 17 JOAs in operation in the United States (Newspaper Association of America, 1994). Currently the largest cities with JOAs include San Francisco, Detroit, Seattle, Cincinnati and Nash-ville.

The Newspaper Preservation Act has been highly controversial since its inception, and has been repeatedly challenged in the courts as to the manner in which the Act has been both implemented and interpreted (see Picard, 1993; Watkins, 1990). The act permits the Attorney General of the United States to allow new JOAs, provided that one of the newspapers is "in probable danger" of failing (Watkins, 1990). In the 1980s, two major judicial challenges concerned the approval of JOAs in Seattle and Detroit. In both cases, the courts allowed the JOAs to remain. With the exception of those papers engaged in JOAs, all newspapers are subject to antitrust laws that prohibit anti-competitive practices and behavior.

Concerns over the increasing size of major newspaper chains, concentra-tion of control and foreign ownership remain important issues in the newspaper industry. To date, no significant legislative actions have been introduced by policymakers.

Technological Forces Affecting Newspapers

Newspapers have been greatly affected by technological changes in the way papers are prepared, printed and distributed. Over the past thirty years, a number of new technologies have impacted the newspaper industry. Perhaps the most significant of these changes was the shift from the old Linotype (also referred to as hot type) method of typesetting to the use of cold type made possible with computer-linked video display terminals (VDTs). As is the case with many industries, newspapers have been revolutionized by advances in computer technology.

Picard (1993) claims that new technologies have had two major effects on the newspaper industry. First, a newspaper can be produced today with fewer employees thanks to sophisticated technology. Departments can directly enter stories and advertisements without the use of typesetters. Many news and syndicated features are distributed in electronic form, and can simply be plugged in to the proper layout position on a page. Second, the newspaper can be produced much faster, allowing for longer deadlines and the ability to provide late-breaking news coverage. This has enabled newspapers to remain more competitive with the electronic media in their ability to cover the news.

Photojournalism has also been affected. Many newspapers can now process photographs directly from the camera, using electronic darkrooms equipped with the appropriate computer hardware and software. Newspapers now have the ability to use digital processing to provide sharper, clearer pictures.

Other new enhancements are expected, particularly in regard to composition and printing technology (Picard, 1993). There are positive and negative aspects of adopting new technologies in newspaper production. On the plus side, newspapers can be created more efficiently, with faster processing and distribution. On the down side, new technologies usually require significant outlays of capital, in turn requiring several months or even years to recapture the return on investment. As such, newspaper managers must weigh the benefits against the anticipated costs when considering new technologies.

The Economic Future of the Newspaper Industry

Although newspapers remain the most profitable form of mass media in the United States, there are concerns about the economic future of the newspaper industry. Although circulation data paint a very favorable picture of newspaper use, the fact is that fewer members of the population are reading newspapers today. Picard (1993) points out that although newspaper circulation grew nearly 19 percent between 1950 and 1990, the nation's population increased by 70 percent. As a result, newspaper penetration has actually declined over time. A growing number of younger people (those under age 18) have little interest in reading a newspaper. Likewise, those Americans who either can't read or cannot read very well, will use the electronic media for the bulk of their news and information.

Another continuing problem for the newspaper industry is the cost of newsprint, which has almost quadrupled in price since 1970 (see Table 11-6). Some newsprint producers were ready to increase prices as much as 10 percent in 1995, which would in turn have a major impact on newspaper profits (Chipello, 1994). Recycling of newspapers has helped curb newsprint costs, but suppliers claim increases are needed in order to maintain profits in their (newsprint) industry.

In order to counter some of the problems within the newspaper industry, publishers are looking for additional markets to develop alternative revenue streams. Many newspapers have expanded their news distribution capabilities by offering voice information services and computer on-line services to customers. Voice services include a variety of information categories, many of which are supported by advertising. Fax information services, 900-number services and other products are quickly expanding the core newspaper business. The Newspaper Association of America estimates that over 150 daily newspapers provide some type of on-line access to their newspapers (Newspaper Association of America, 1994). Other companies, such as Times Mirror, are focusing on different means to distribute information-based products via CD-ROM through alternative forms of electronic publishing (Rose, 1994).

The newspaper industry is expected to grow at a rate of 5.4 percent through

Table 11-6. Newsprint prices

Year	Price* (per metric ton)
1970	$ 179
1971	188
1972	194
1973	235
1974	259
1975	287
1976	336
1977	336
1978	353
1979	413
1980	440
1981	500
1982	469
1983	500
1984	535
1985	535
1986	570
1987	610
1988	650
1989	650
1990	685
1991	685
1992	685
1993	685

*Prices cited in effect at year end, converted to 30-pound basis weight; end-of-year West Coast price was $630 per ton.

1997 (Veronis, Suhler and Associates, 1994). Veronis, Suhler and Associates expects newspaper advertising to reach $40 billion by 1997, and overall newspaper revenues (combined daily, Sunday and weekly circulation and advertising) to reach $56.8 billion by 1997. Daily newspapers will continue to attract the largest share of revenues through 1997.

Summary

The newspaper industry is one of the oldest forms of mass media in the United States. Newspapers play an important role in society as a source of news and information, as well as a commercial entity linking advertisers and consumers.

As an industry, newspapers remain as the most profitable of all mass media industries, although the gap separating newspapers and television has diminished over the past few years. Newspapers draw revenues from national, retail and classified advertising, as well as through daily and Sunday circulation. Daily and evening papers have declined over the past several years. Weekly papers have flourished, reflecting the population shift of households to the suburbs and the desire for local news in the suburban communities in which they reside.

Most daily newspapers are part of large chains. Among the leading newspapers publishers in the United States are Gannett, Knight-Ridder, Thomson, Newhouse and Times Mirror. The majority of cities in the United States are served by a single newspaper, enabling most newspapers to operate under a monopolistic market structure. Economies of scope exist in newspaper production, circulation and advertising, creating significant barriers to entry for new competitors. As such, newspaper markets tend to be heavily concentrated.

Newspapers are subject to few regulations at either the local, state or federal level. The 1970 Newspaper Preservation Act allows a failing newspaper to combine operations with a stronger competitor in forming JOAs. Under a JOA, editorial departments are separated, but all other departments are consolidated. Controversy has been created in the newspaper industry by JOAs, but they have kept several papers from ceasing operation.

New technology is changing the way newspapers are created, distributed and consumed. Many newspapers have started on-line services to allow computer users to access different types of information. Rising costs of newsprint have caused concern in the industry. Newspapers continue seeking ways to expand by offering new products in expanding markets.

Discussion Questions

1. What factors have led to a decline in the number of daily newspapers?
2. What factors have led to an increase in the number of weekly or suburban papers?
3. Discuss the three types of advertising found in the newspaper industry. Which category is the most important to daily newspapers?
4. Discuss the following terms as they relate to the newspaper industry: (a) *chains*; (b) *retail trading zone* or *RTZ*; (c) *joint operating agreement* or *JOA*.
5. To what extent do foreign companies own or control U.S. newspapers? Should policymakers be concerned about increasing foreign ownership of newspapers? Why or why not?

Exercises

1. Compare copies of the local daily paper(s) serving your market to the weekly suburban paper(s) serving your market in regard to the following criteria: (a) amount of space devoted to news; (b) amount of space devoted to advertising; (c) types of advertising found in each paper; and (d) circulation.
2. Obtain a copy of *USA Today* and *The New York Times.* How are these two papers

similar to each other? How are they different? Describe the type of audience each paper serves.

3. Make arrangements to visit a local newspaper. Write a summary of your experiences, noting in particular what you observed in the way of technological enhancements used in producing the paper.

4. Arrange a guest speaker from your local newspaper—ideally a reporter or someone involved in the editorial department.

References

Chipello, C. J. (1994). Newsprint producers push for more price increases. *The Wall Street Journal*, August 25, p. B3.

Dertouzous, J. N. and Trautman, W. B. (1990). Economic effect of media concentration: Estimates from a model of the newspaper firm. *The Journal of Industrial Economics* 39:1–14.

Gustafsson, K. E. (1978). The circulation spiral and the principle of household coverage. *The Scandinavian Economic History Review* 26:1–14.

Litman, B. R. (1988). Microeconomic foundations. In: Picard, R. G., McCombs, M., Winter, J. P., and Lacy, S. (eds.). *Press Concentration and Monopoly: New Perspectives on Newspaper Ownership and Operation*. Norwood, NJ: Ablex Publishing Company, pp. 3–34.

Newspaper Association of America (1994). *Facts About Newspapers*. Reston, VA: Newspaper Association of America.

Picard, R. G. (1988a). Measures of concentration in the daily newspaper industry. *Journal of Media Economics* 1(1):61–74.

Picard, R. G. (1988b). Pricing behavior of newspapers. In: Picard, R. G., McCombs, M., Winter, J. P., and Lacy, S. (eds.). *Press Concentration and Monopoly: New Perspectives on Newspaper Ownership and Operation*. Norwood, NJ: Ablex Publishing Company, pp. 55–69.

Picard, R. G. (1993). Economics of the daily newspaper industry. In: Alexander, A., Owers, J., and Carveth, R. (eds.). *Media Economics: Theory and Practice*. New York: Lawrence Erlbaum Associates, pp. 181–204.

Rose, F. (1994). Digital turnabout. *The Wall Street Journal,* June 6, A1, A6.

Rosse, J. N. and Dertouzous, J. N. (1979). The evolution of one newspaper cities. In: Federal Trade Commission, *Proceedings of the Symposium on Media Concentration*, vol. 2. Washington, D C: Government Printing Office, pp. 429–471.

Veronis, Suhler and Associates (1994). *Communications Industry Report*. New York: Veronis, Suhler and Associates.

Vivian, J. (1995). *The Media of Mass Communication*, 3rd ed. Needham Heights, MA: Allyn & Bacon.

Watkins, J. J. (1990). *The Mass Media and the Law*. Englewood Cliffs, NJ: Prentice-Hall.

Wirth, M. O. (1986). Economic barriers to entering media industries in the United States. In: McLaughlin, M. (ed.). *Communication Yearbook*, 9. Beverly Hills: Sage, pp. 423–442.

12

THE MAGAZINE INDUSTRY

In this chapter you will:

- Identify some of the major players, market structure and economic characteristics of the magazine industry.

- Learn the two types of divisions in magazine publishing.

- Understand the various markets for magazines.

- Learn how technology is changing the magazine industry.

- Understand why the magazine industry is expanding into international publishing.

Magazines have been an important source of news, information and literature in the United States since the early 1800s. Magazines have contributed to the transmission of culture, while introducing new journalistic approaches and innovations to the American public (Vivian, 1995). As a visual medium, magazines have captured history in their pages. Articles and photographs have informed generations of readers from the Civil War to the Gulf War, charting the growth of America and the collapse of Communism.

The growth of magazines as a mass medium provided those who could not afford the high price of books the opportunity to read literature from some of the great authors of the world. Magazines such as *The Saturday Evening Post, The New Yorker, Atlantic, Look, Life* and *Reader's Digest* are but a few of the magazines that have educated and influenced thousands of readers throughout their publishing history.

Magazine publishing is the work of two separate divisions (Worthington,

1994). The business side handles all of the business aspects of the publication, including such areas as marketing, advertising, finance and personnel. The editorial side is charged with producing the magazine, and encompasses all of the editors, writers, photographers, graphic artists and other personnel needed to create the magazine.

Magazines have changed and adapted through the years, along with other forms of mass media. Magazines no longer attract large, national audiences as they did in the pre-television world. Today the magazine industry is specialized, with most publishers targeting smaller markets of readers. Vivian (1995) uses the term *demassification* to describe how the magazine industry increasingly is targeting audiences with products designed to meet specific interests and needs. Evidence of this trend is found in the number of magazine titles published in the United States. The Magazine Publishers of America estimates that over eleven thousand magazines are published in the United States each year (Standard & Poor's, 1994).

The magazine industry has experienced sluggish growth in circulation (readership) and advertising during the 1990s. A poor domestic economy in the early 1990s negatively impacted advertising and circulation sales. An improving economic picture should provide some growth for the industry through the end of the century.

Magazines draw revenues from two important sources. Advertisers represent the largest source of revenue for the magazine industry. According to Veronis, Suhler and Associates (1994), magazine advertising accounts for approximately 56 percent of industry revenues compared with 44 percent for circulation. Circulation revenues are obtained from consumers who purchase magazines through annual subscriptions or via newsstand sales. Individual newsstand copies are usually priced higher than an annual subscription, and account for approximately 20 percent of total circulation revenues in the magazine industry (*U.S. Industrial Outlook,* 1994).

Magazines compete for audiences and advertisers of other forms of publishing, as well as of the electronic media. With numerous choices available for advertisers and growing leisure-time options for consumers, magazine publishers are aggressively pursuing new products and revenue streams to supplement traditional publishing.

The Market for Magazines

As with other media industries, the magazine industry operates in several different markets. Magazines can be broken into identifiable submarkets, such as the markets for particular categories of magazines (i.e., consumer magazines, business/trade magazines and professional journals). We could also consider the time frame—whether published as a monthly, bimonthly or weekly—of individual publications as separate markets. Finally, we could consider the U.S. national market as compared with international markets.

The magazine industry could also be analyzed by examining the market for advertisers, as well as the market for publishing (acquisition of magazines by other publishers). Because of the number of potential submarkets to consider, and in order not to make the examination too tedious, this section will focus on the market for magazines in three broad categories: (a) the consumer market, which will encompass all types of magazines; (b) the market for magazine advertising; and (c) the market or demand for magazine publishing.

Consumer demand for magazines. Although total magazine circulation has been somewhat flat during the 1990s, Americans still read magazines on a regular basis. According to studies by the Magazine Research Institute, the more education and income a person has, the greater the individual's likelihood to read magazines (*U.S. Industrial Outlook,* 1994). Most readers subscribe to the magazines they prefer; single-copy sales have fallen over the past decade. Still, some magazines have considerable success with single-copy issues such as the annual *Sports Illustrated* swimsuit edition, and *Playboy*'s annual Playmate of the Year issue (Standard & Poor's, 1994).

Consumer, or general interest, magazines are the most visible to readers. *Modern Maturity* is the leading monthly consumer magazine in the Unites States in terms of total circulation. Other leading magazines include *Reader's Digest, TV Guide, National Geographic, Better Homes and Gardens, Good Housekeeping, Ladies Home Journal* and *Family Circle* (see Table 12-1). New magazines

Table 12-1. Magazine circulation leaders

Rank	Magazine Title	Circulation
1	*Modern Maturity*	22,399,000
2	*Reader's Digest*	16,261,968
3	*TV Guide*	14,122,915
4	*National Geographic*	9,390,787
5	*Better Homes and Gardens*	7,600,960
6	*Good Housekeeping*	5,162,597
7	*Ladies Home Journal*	5,153,565
8	*Family Circle*	5,114,030
9	*The Cable Guide*	4,860,703
10	*Woman's Day*	4,858,625
11	*McCall's*	4,605,441
12	*Time*	4,103,772
13	*People Weekly*	3,446,569
14	*National Enquirer*	3,403,330
15	*Playboy*	3,402,617
16	*AAA World*	3,400,807
17	*Sports Illustrated*	3,356,729
18	*Redbook*	3,345,451
19	*Prevention*	3,220,763
20	*Newsweek*	3,156,192

Source: Adapted from Circulation overview (1995).

have appeared with increasing frequency during the 1990s; records for new start-up magazines were established in 1991 (553), 1992 (679) and 1993 (789) (Standard & Poor's, 1994). According to Vivian (1995), only one of every five new magazines survives into its third year of publishing.

There are magazines for virtually every demographic age group, lifestyle and hobby. The best areas for growth in the industry are magazines that specialize further into specific lifestyles and interests. Among the likely targets are children, youth, senior citizens, baby boomers and ethnic groups. For example, several new magazines are targeting the so-called "Generation X" group of young adults in their twenties. Recent publications targeted to this demographic group include *Axcess, Might* and *Swing* (Keeton, 1994). Other publications target second-generation ethnic minorities, such as *A. Magazine* and *Onward*, which are aimed at Asian-Americans (Mehta, 1994).

Prices for magazines have remained relatively stable over the past few years, averaging no more than a 5 percent increase. Table 12-2 charts the number of magazines published in the United States for selected years, along with the average copy and subscription price. Prices for both single copies and subscriptions are not expected to rise more than 2–3 percent per year over the next few years, although new postal increases (as in 1995) usually force an increase in subscription rates for magazines.

Table 12-2. Magazine industry statistics

Year	Average Number of U.S. Periodicals	Average Single-copy Price	Yearly Subscription Price
1993	10,857	$ 2.95	$ 28.50
1992	11,143	2.85	27.00
1991	11,239	2.66	26.74
1990	11,092	2.65	27.11
1989	11,556	2.48	25.96
1988	11,229	2.29	25.29
1987	11,593	2.20	24.45
1986	11,328	2.20	23.24
1985	11,090	2.10	23.15
1984	10,809	2.05	22.37

Source: Modified from Standard & Poor's (1994).

Demand for magazine advertising. Of all dollars spent on advertising in the United States, magazine advertising has averaged around 5.4 percent of total advertising revenues since 1986. Advertising revenue for all magazines totaled $7.625 billion in 1993; revenues are expected to reach just slightly over $8 billion in 1995 (Veronis, Suhler and Associates, 1994).

Magazine advertising is dominated by ten categories that account for approximately 74 percent of total magazine advertising. The top categories, based on complete 1993 data (Standard & Poor's, 1994), include automotive (14 percent), cosmetics and toiletries (11 percent), direct response (10 percent), business and consumer services (8 percent), footwear and accessories (7 percent), food (6 percent), computers and office equipment (5 percent), travel and hotels (5 percent), drugs (5 percent) and media and publishing (5 percent). The number of pages devoted to advertising has grown among in-flight magazines, home magazines and general-interest titles, while declining in Sunday magazines, youth, metropolitan and civic titles (Standard & Poor's, 1994).

Demand for magazines—acquisitions. Publishing mergers and acquisitions operated at a frenzied pace through much of the 1980s. According to data compiled by Greco (1993), some 584 transactions took place, with several major U.S. periodicals (e.g., *The New Yorker, U.S. News & World Report, TV Guide*) changing ownership during this time. News Corporation's acquisition of *TV Guide, Seventeen* and *The Daily Racing Form* for three billion dollars in 1988 represents the largest magazine transactions to date (Greco, 1993).

A downward economy slowed transactions in the magazine industry during the 1990s. Major acquisitions include Conde Nast Publications, which purchased Knapp Communications, publishers of *Architectural Digest* and *Bon Appetit* for $170 million in 1993 (*U.S. Industrial Outlook,* 1994); and the 1994 acquisition of *McCall's* and *Family Circle* by Gruner + Jahr (a German company) from the New York Times Company for $325 million in 1994 (Reilly, 1994).

Major Players in the Magazine Industry

There are numerous publishers in the magazine industry, ranging from large-scale international conglomerates to small publishing houses producing single publications. The major firms operating in the magazine industry are listed in Table 12-3. Time Warner is the largest publisher of magazines in the United States, and owns several popular consumer titles such as *Time, Life, Fortune, Money, People, Sports Illustrated* and *Entertainment Weekly.*

Other major U.S. publishers include Hearst (*Good Housekeeping, Esquire* and *Cosmopolitan*), the New York Times Company (*Tennis, Golf World*), Meredith (*Better Homes and Gardens, Ladies' Home Journal*) and Conde Nast (*Gourmet, Conde Nast Traveler, Architectural Digest* and *Bon Appetit*). Major overseas publishers of popular U.S. magazines include Hachette SA (*Woman's Day, Elle, Car and Driver*), Gruner + Jahr (*McCall's* and *Family Circle*) and News Corporation (*TV Guide, Mirabella*).

Table 12-3. Top 10 magazine publishers (listed by Jan.–Sept. ad revenues, millions of dollars)

Name	PIB Revenues 1993	% of Total PIB 1993
Time Warner	$ 1,044.6	17.9
Hearst Magazines	511.8	8.8
Conde Nast Publications	475.4	8.1
New York Times Co.	406.4	7.0
Parade Publications	305.7	5.2
Meredith Corp.	278.5	4.8
Hachette SA	263.1	4.5
News Corp.	244.8	4.2
Times Mirror Magazines	172.8	3.0
Newsweek Inc.	168.3	2.5

Source: Modified from Standard & Poor's (1994).

Note: PIB, or Publishers Information Bureau, compiles revenues on approximately 190 leading U.S. magazines. Percent of revenue totals are only for PIB-measured periodicals, and do not reflect total industry revenues.

Market Structure

The magazine industry operates under a monopolistic competitive market structure. Remember that in a monopolistic competitive market structure, there are many sellers offering products that are similar, but are not perfect substitutes for one another. This definition best describes the magazine industry.

The large number of individual publishers suggests there will be several titles geared toward specific interests, yet each is somewhat unique in its presentation. The prices paid for magazines (see Table 12-2) also indicate a monopolistic competitive structure; if magazines operated as an oligopoly, prices would likely have risen at a higher rate, assuming a lack of reasonable substitutes. It is unlikely that the magazine industry will move away from a monopolistic competitive structure in the immediate future.

Market Concentration

No studies have been identified that examine concentration in the magazine industry. In order to get an approximate measure of concentration in the magazine industry, the author calculated the top four (CR4) and top eight (CR8) concentration ratios using the data from 1993 found in Table 12-3.

The CR4 ratio measured 31 percent, whereas the CR8 ratio was calculated to be 44 percent. Recall that in Chapter 4, a market was considered concentrated if the CR4 ratio was equal to or larger than 50 percent and the CR8 was equal to or larger than 75 percent. Although this analysis is limited to just one year of data, the measures indicate that the magazine industry is not concentrated. We could anticipate similar findings using the Herfindahl-Hirschman Index (HHI) because, with a large number of publishers, the individual market shares would be quite small when squared and added together. The low level of concentration in the magazine industry is another indication that the industry operates under a monopolistic competitive market structure.

Regulatory Forces Impacting the Magazine Industry

Magazines are not subject to any direct governmental regulation beyond that imposed on any other business operating in the United States (e.g., wages, taxes, employment and labor acts). There have been continuing concerns in Washington over the issue of recycling, particularly as it pertains to the magazine industry. Some publishers have made the switch to printing on recycled paper, and others will eventually follow suit. However, recycled paper is limited in supply, has a higher cost and is considered lower quality than new paper stock.

In 1993, the Environmental Protection Agency (EPA) revised its guidelines regarding the acquisition of recycled paper by governmental agencies. Magazine publishers were concerned at the time that the EPA would adopt mandatory printing requirements that would likely become the same standards used in magazine publishing (*U.S. Industrial Outlook,* 1994). To date, no further EPA actions have been taken, although environmental issues remain an important issue in society.

Technological Forces Impacting Magazines

Technology is creating exciting changes in the magazine industry. Computer technology has decreased the time needed for publishing and has reduced the number of people needed to produce a magazine. Downsizing led to a loss of jobs in magazine publishing during the 1990s, in part due to technology, but also because of a sluggish economy. The entire magazine industry now employs slightly over 110,000 people (*U.S. Industrial Outlook,* 1994). According to Worthington (1994), it is now possible for a single graphic artist and one editor to produce a 100-page monthly magazine using freelance writers.

Emerging technology is allowing magazines to be produced in new electronic and interactive formats, which publishers hope will lead to new readers and revenue streams. Many publishers, including Time Warner, have created on-line editions of their magazines through the World Wide Web (WWW). The Time Warner service, known as Pathfinder, allows Internet users to read articles from publications such as *Time*, *Sports Illustrated* and *Entertainment Weekly*, and to exchange messages with the publisher and other readers (Carmody, 1994; Ziegler, 1994). Scores of other publishers (e.g., Hearst, Ziff-Davis, IDG Communications, Conde Nast, Hachette and Times Mirror) are moving rapidly to publish electronic versions on the Internet to attract new readers and revenues.

Other publishers are pursuing CD-ROM magazine formats. CD-ROM versions enable magazines to include full-motion video and sound clips in addition to text and graphics. What is not clear is the consumer demand for electronic and interactive magazine versions. These new formats offer features superior to printed editions, but also lack the portability, photography, tables, illustrations and other artwork available in print (Standard & Poor's, 1994). Most likely, electronic versions will attract new magazine readers as opposed to existing readers, thereby opening up new markets for publishers.

Magazine publishers are also finding more utility for their subscriber databases. Publishers are building more comprehensive profiles of their readers. These profiles are used in turn to better position advertising and other products of interest (Department of Commerce). Coupled with electronic magazines and interactivity between publisher and subscriber, many creative marketing applications are possible.

Several magazine publishers have entered joint ventures with other companies to produce new products. Custom publishing, combining the increasing technical capabilities of information with a growing consumer use of computer technology, will lead to more partnerships between publishers and other companies interested in developing magazines for their audiences. For example, IBM and the New York Times Company are partners in publishing *Profit* and *Beyond Computing*, and Gruner+ Jahr is working with the retailer Target to publish *Target the Family* (*U.S. Industrial Outlook,* 1994).

The Economic Future of the Magazine Industry

Magazine publishers face a challenging future as they attempt to hold on to both advertisers and consumers, control costs and enter new technological markets and international publishing opportunities. Publishers will be faced with meeting the demands of both advertisers and readers amid growing competition from other publishers and the electronic media.

Magazines that cater to narrowly targeted audiences will be more attractive to advertisers in the immediate future. Publishers will continue to hone and improve the quality of their editorial divisions to be certain they are providing readers with material that serves their needs.

International publishing opportunities provide additional markets for U.S. magazines, and this area will continue to expand. Most of the activity in international markets is occurring in Europe, Latin America, the Middle East, Asia and Africa (Standard & Poor's, 1994). Fewer efforts are being directed at Eastern Europe, Canada and countries in the Pacific Rim. The numerous special-interest titles produced by American publishers have found favor in many countries where the economy only supports broader-based, national magazines. American publishers also benefit from the fact that English is understood in most parts of the world, resulting in reduced language barriers for readers.

Veronis, Suhler and Associates projects magazine revenue by separating consumer and business titles. Consumer magazine advertising is expected to reach $10.3 billion by 1997, and consumer spending on magazines should reach $7.5 billion, for a consumer total of $17.8 billion (Veronis, Suhler and Associates, 1994). Business magazines are expected to generate $5 billion in advertising and another $2.4 billion from users, for a total of $7.4 billion in 1997. Total consumer and business magazine revenues are expected to reach $26.9 billion in 1997, reflecting an estimated 6 percent growth rate (Veronis, Suhler and Associates, 1994).

Summary

Magazines have played an important role in entertaining, educating and informing Americans since the early 1800s. Magazine publishing is accomplished through the combined efforts of two divisions. The business division handles all business aspects, while the editorial division handles the actual creation of the magazine. Over the years, the magazine industry has evolved into a specialized industry serving readers with a number of specific interests.

Magazines draw revenues from two sources: advertisers and circulation. Advertising accounts for approximately 55 percent of revenues, and circulation consists of subscriptions and individual copy sales. The magazine industry can be analyzed in terms of three markets: the consumer market, the advertising market and the market for the actual publications.

The magazine industry operates in a monopolistic competitive market structure. Several major firms (e.g., Time Warner, Hearst, Conde Nast, Hachette) hold key positions in the magazine industry, but no single firm or set of firms dominates the market.

No significant regulation impacts the market, although publishers have been concerned about the possibility of mandated use of recycled paper in magazine publishing. In terms of technology, the magazine industry is rapidly developing new markets for magazines through electronic editions and CD-ROM formats. Key questions remain as to the demand by users for electronic magazine versions.

In the years ahead, magazine publishers will try to maintain market share, control costs and seek expansion by entering new markets and creating and marketing new products. International publishing opportunities will also help industry revenues. Domestic revenues for advertising and circulation are projected to grow at a rate of 6 percent through 1997.

Discussion Questions

1. How has the magazine industry changed during its history? What sort of new changes is the magazine industry likely to encounter?
2. Identify and discuss the revenue sources for magazines.
3. Describe the magazine industry in terms of market structure. How concentrated is the magazine industry?
4. Discuss the following terms as they relate to the magazine industry: *demassification, editorial* and *electronic versions*.
5. To what extent do foreign companies own or control U.S. magazines? Should policymakers be concerned about increasing foreign ownership of magazines? Why or why not?

Exercises

1. Compare copies of magazines found in your household with respect to the following criteria: (a) types of editorial content; (b) types of advertisers; (c) audiences likely to read the magazine; and (d) publisher.
2. Compare a "hard" copy of a magazine with its electronic version on the Internet. How are they different? How are they similar? Describe the contents of each magazine.
3. At a newsstand or other retailer that carries a number of magazines, identify how many magazine titles exist for a particular hobby or interest. Examine these magazines to try and determine how they are unique from one another. Also compare the cost, number of pages and publisher of each title.
4. Arrange to have a graphic artist, freelance writer or other member of a magazine staff visit your class as a guest speaker to gain their insight on magazine publishing.

References

Carmody, D. (1994). Time Inc. stakes out front-line multimedia position. *The Dallas Morning News*, October 24, p. 4D.

Circulation overview (1995). *Folio: Special Sourcebook Issue,* pp. 161–163.

Greco, A. N. (1993). Publishing economics: Mergers and acquisitions in the U.S. Publishing Industry: 1980–1989. In: Alexander, A., Owers, J., and Carveth, R. (eds.). *Media Economics: Theory and Practice.* New York: Lawrence Erlbaum Associates, pp. 205–224.

Keeton, L. E. (1994). New magazines aim to reach (and rechristen) Generation X. *The Wall Street Journal*, October 17, pp. B1, B7.

Mehta, S. N. (1994). New magazines target U.S.-born ethnic minorities. *The Wall Street Journal*, July 26, p. B2.

Reilly, P. M. (1994). German publishing executive rolls up his sleeves at McCall's. *The Wall Street Journal*, September 12, pp. B1, B6.

Standard & Poor's (1994). *Standard & Poor's Industry Surveys.* New York: Standard & Poor's.

U.S. Industrial Outlook. (1994). Washington, DC: U.S. Department of Commerce.

Veronis, Suhler and Associates (1994). *Communications Industry Report.* New York: Veronis, Suhler and Associates.

Vivian, J. (1995). *The Media of Mass Communication*, 3rd ed. Needham Heights, MA: Allyn & Bacon.

Worthington, R. (1994). Research review: Magazine management and economics. *Electronic Journal of Communication* 4(2–4). Communication Institute for Online Scholarship, Inc.

Ziegler, B. (1994, October 24). Time Warner Inc. puts its magazines on the Internet. *The Wall Street Journal,* p. B5.

13

THE BOOK INDUSTRY

In this chapter you will:

- Identify some of the major players, market structure and economic characteristics of the book industry.

- Identify the various markets for books.

- Recognize how the demand for books is a combination of many macroeconomic and microeconomic variables.

- Learn how technology is expanding the market for books through nonprint formats.

- Understand why international revenues are likely to grow in the years ahead.

The book industry has the distinction of being the first true mass medium in history, made possible by the invention of moveable type by Johannes Gutenberg, which historians believed happened around 1446 (Vivian, 1995). The printing process that Gutenberg invented quickly spread throughout Europe and other developing nations. The ability to mass produce the printed word revolutionized communication and literally changed the world. It made information available to the common people that previously had been held only by the privileged few. The same basic processes used in printing books would later expand into the publishing of newspapers and magazines.

Today, the book industry remains a very important industry, with total 1993 revenues exceeding $17.2 billion (*U.S. Industrial Outlook,* 1994). Like many other mass media industries, the book industry faces many challenges in the coming years as it tries to maintain consumer interest and market share in petition with other forms of leisure activities, and as it continues expansion into nonprint markets.

The book industry draws revenues primarily from the sale of books to different categories of buyers such as consumer, educational, business and institutional (library) purchasers. Most consumer books are purchased by individuals through various types of bookstores, whereas textbooks (educational books) are acquired by colleges and universities, state education boards and local school districts. Unlike many media industries, the book industry is not dependent on advertising for revenues.

It is estimated that more than 50,000 new books are published each year in the United States, and that the average American purchases at least one book per year (Standard & Poor's, 1994; *U.S. Industrial Outlook,* 1994). As such, retailing and marketing are critical functions of book publishers.

Book publishers range from large media conglomerates to small, specialty publishers. Over the past 30 years, many smaller publishers have been acquired by larger companies. International publishers have established a strong presence in the United States, and United States-based publishers are also pursuing opportunities in marketing books to other countries of the world in both traditional and nonprint formats.

Demand for books is influenced by several microeconomic and macroeconomic factors. In the United States, the state of the economy, educational enrollments, household disposable income, professional employment, and institutional and library funding are some of the key variables that impact the demand for books (*U.S. Industrial Outlook,* 1994). In the international arena, the demand for books is related to many factors, including currency exchange rates, literacy rates, occupational status and English fluency.

Although the book industry may be the oldest of the mass media industries covered in this text, it is by no means static and resistant to change. As this chapter illustrates, book publishing is evolving and adapting in order to remain competitive in a growing, media-saturated environment.

The Market for Books

The book industry can be broken into several markets for analysis. Most industry sources examine the book publishing industry in three broad categories: consumer (also called trade) books, professional books and educational books (textbooks). In analyzing the market for books, this chapter will follow a similar approach, reviewing the demand for consumer, business and educational books, as well as the demand for book publishers.

Demand for consumer books. Consumer book sales consist of the following areas: adult trade, juvenile trade, religious, book clubs, mail order, mass-market paperbacks, university press and subscription reference. Books published and total sales figures for consumer books are listed in Table 13-1. As the table illustrates, the total sales of consumer books have risen steadily every year, reaching an estimated $14.4 billion in 1993.

The adult trade category is the largest in the consumer book market, accounting for approximately 30 percent of all consumer book sales (Standard & Poor's, 1994). Within the adult trade category, most of the sales represent adult fiction, advice and how-to books. Juvenile trade book sales have declined in the past few years, perhaps reflecting more interest in other forms of leisure entertainment such as toys and video games. Adult and juvenile trade books reached $3.6 billion in sales in 1993 (*U.S. Industrial Outlook,* 1994).

One other interesting phenomenon noted in Table 13-1 is the gradual decline in mass market paperbacks. Consumers apparently are buying more hardcover books, reflecting the trend in discounting hardcover editions by major book retailers such as Waldenbooks, Barnes & Noble, Crown and B. Dalton. Paberback publishers are now concentrating on original works in popular subjects through romance, westerns, mysteries and military themes.

A growing trend in book retailing and marketing involves the development of book superstores, which feature inventories of thirty thousand to one hundred fifty thousand titles compared with the average mall bookstore, which carries about twenty thousand titles (Standard & Poor's, 1994). Over three hundred superstores will be in operation by the end of 1995, and many of the stores feature a variety of amenities for shoppers such as couches and recliners for reading, a refreshment area and play areas for small children. Staffs at the superstores tend to be more knowledgeable and specialized in particular areas, increasing the level of service demanded by customers. Further, most superstores are equipped with computer search capabilities to locate easily titles that customers desire.

Demand for professional books. Professional book publishing includes the categories of business, law and medicine, as well as technical and scientific books. The number of books published and total sales figures for professional books are listed in Table 13-2. As the table illustrates, the total sales of professional books have also grown every year, reaching an estimated $3.05 billion in 1993.

Among the types of books that contribute heavily to professional book sales are computer, software and medical publications (Standard & Poor's, 1994). Growth in professional employment and an increase in the number of college-educated adults have also stimulated demand for professional books. Business and legal publication shipments were negatively impacted by the sluggish economy in the early 1990s, but these categories are expected to rebound in the immediate future. Society's concern over health care and the "graying" of the U.S. population will continue the demand for medical books.

Table 13-1. Consumer book sales (millions of books/millions of dollars)

Year	Adult Trade	Juvenile Trade	Religious	Book Clubs	Mail Order	Mass-market Paperbacks	University Press	Subscription Reference	Total Books	Total Sales
1993	472.0	315.0	137.0	105.0	110.0	430.0	15.0	0.9	1,584.9	14,368.0
1992	445.0	318.0	135.0	104.0	112.0	435.0	14.8	0.9	1,564.7	13,424.5
1991	412.6	324.0	132.7	109.2	132.4	448.2	14.6	0.9	1,574.6	12,729.0
1990	403.1	301.4	129.8	108.0	137.6	432.9	13.9	1.0	1,527.7	11,819.2
1989	403.7	281.2	124.2	109.1	152.3	441.0	13.6	1.0	1,526.1	11,214.4
1988	365.3	244.4	120.7	112.3	137.8	418.9	13.1	1.0	1,413.5	9,823.4
1987	357.3	219.5	127.8	120.6	128.3	391.0	13.1	1.0	1,358.6	8,886.2
1986	352.3	210.3	132.9	125.8	124.2	381.1	14.4	1.0	1,342.0	7,920.7
1985	359.9	192.6	133.5	129.6	121.1	381.5	14.5	0.9	1,333.6	7,576.5
1984	340.6	179.1	149.0	133.8	111.5	388.9	14.4	0.9	1,318.2	6,922.1
1983	340.2	166.1	149.1	134.4	128.6	377.6	15.0	0.9	1,311.9	6,566.2

Source: Standard & Poor's (1994).

Table 13-2. *Production and sale of professional books (millions of books/millions of dollars)*

Year	Business	Law	Medicine	Technical, Scientific	Total Books	Business	Law	Medicine	Medicine	Technical, Scientific	Total Sales
1992	37.7	22.8	16.4	73.5	150.4	$ 550.0	$ 1,050.0	$ 620.0		$ 830.0	$ 3,050.0
1991	35.7	22.1	15.8	71.7	145.3	502.9	972.1	567.8		783.9	2,826.7
1990	38.7	22.5	15.4	72.0	148.6	527.9	947.5	526.3		764.2	2,765.9
1989	36.8	22.0	15.0	71.5	145.3	481.7	883.0	490.5		737.6	2,592.8
1988	35.1	21.6	14.9	70.4	142.0	446.0	833.0	445.9		687.0	2,411.9
1987	32.8	20.7	14.5	67.9	135.9	388.8	780.0	406.5		632.0	2,207.3
1986	30.6	19.9	14.3	67.8	132.6	352.5	732.4	390.1		601.5	2,076.5
1985	27.6	18.6	13.8	65.7	125.7	321.3	685.8	363.6		557.3	1,928.0
1984	25.2	17.5	13.4	64.4	120.5	284.1	639.7	342.6		538.9	1,805.3
1983	25.5	18.3	14.4	70.1	128.3	258.0	606.4	320.1		518.6	1,703.1

Source: Standard & Poor's (1994).
Note: Publishers' sales reflect sales to retailers and include exports.

Demand for educational books. The market for educational or textbooks can be broken into two separate submarkets: the market for elementary-high school books (referred to as "elhi" in the book industry) and the market for college textbooks. Sales figures for both elhi and college textbooks are listed in Table 13-3. In 1993, the combined sale of elhi and college textbooks was expected to reach $4.575 billion.

Table 13-3. *Sales of educational books (millions of books/millions of dollars)*

Year	Elhi	College	Total Books	Elhi	College	Total Sales
1993*	198.0	136.3	334.3	$2,039.4	$2,535.8	$4,575.2
1992	196.0	135.0	331.0	1,942.0	2,437.5	4,379.5
1991	206.0	132.8	338.8	1,973.7	2,325.9	4,299.6
1990	209.3	136.9	346.2	1,947.9	2,319.0	4,266.9
1989	213.2	136.0	349.2	1,908.7	2,144.1	4,052.8
1988	201.8	130.2	332.0	1,716.4	1,997.5	3,713.9
1987	206.8	118.9	325.7	1,632.8	1,802.6	3,435.4
1986	227.8	111.1	338.9	1,534.3	1,670.3	3,204.6
1985	233.8	110.0	343.8	1,415.3	1,575.3	2,990.6
1984	231.1	112.2	343.3	1,259.3	1,508.9	2,768.2
1983	233.0	117.0	350.0	1,124.4	1,477.4	2,601.8

Source: Standard & Poor's (1994).
*1993 data are estimates.

Demand for elhi books is driven by several different factors. State adoption schedules vary for textbooks. California (9.65 percent), Texas (7.74 percent), Florida (4.8 percent) and Indiana (2.81 percent) purchase 25 percent of all elhi textbooks sold in the United States (Standard & Poor's, 1994). Enrollment levels also impact elhi sales. Figures from the National Center for Education Statistics indicate enrollments will rise steadily through the year 2003, averaging around 6 percent a year (Standard & Poor's). School budgets are also critical in assessing demand for elhi books, and local budgets are affected by local tax revenues. Elhi books accounted for approximately 23 percent of all books sold in 1993 (Standard & Poor's, 1994).

Demand for college textbooks is based almost entirely on enrollment. College publishing remains the most profitable form of all book publishing, with costs relatively low and prices relatively high (Standard & Poor's, 1994). However, the growth in the number of nontraditional students has affected both college enrollment and the demand for textbooks. When the economy declines, more workers return to school to improve education and job skills. As the economy grows and creates more job opportunities, enrollment tends to drop, especially for part-time students.

Colleges and universities are also experimenting with new technologies to supplement textbooks. The use of computers, CD-ROM applications, electronic mail and computer conferences all provide alternative means of educating students. Many universities are beginning to invest in distance learning involving audio, video and interactive teleconferencing. How these new technologies may impact the traditional college textbook has yet to be determined.

Demand for book publishers—acquisitions. Mergers and acquisitions among book publishing companies have slowed in recent years, although there were numerous transactions that took place during the 1980s (see Greco, 1993). Most of the acquisitions have involved larger publishers acquiring smaller publishers. Viacom's $10 billion acquisition of Paramount Communications in 1994 included the lucrative Simon and Schuster Publishing Division, and represents one of the biggest publishing-related transaction in the 1990s (Cox and Roberts, 1994).

Demand for publishing acquisitions has slowed primarily because publishers want to avoid higher debt loads (*U.S. Industrial Outlook,* 1994). Publishers appear to be concentrating on maintaining market share and using capital to expand into nonprint markets.

Major Players in the Book Industry

There are over seven hundred book publishers in the book industry, ranging from international media companies to small, specialty publishers. Among the major United States-based publishers are Viacom (Paramount), Reader's Digest Association, Time Warner, Hearst, Newhouse, Times Mirror and General Cinema. Major international publishers and their home locations include A. G. Bertelsmann (Germany), MCA (Japan), News Corporation (Australia) and International Thomson (Canada).

Market Structure

Like the magazine industry, the book industry operates under a monopolistic competitive market structure, as evidenced by the large number of publishers. However, most of the revenues derived in book publishing are absorbed by the companies mentioned earlier in the chapter.

The large number of acquisitions during the 1980s suggested that the book industry was slowly moving toward an oligopolistic structure, raising concern among some critics regarding the overall control of book publishing by both domestic and foreign owners. Although these concerns are not necessarily unfounded, there are no indications that the book publishing industry will move away from a monopolistic competitive structure in the foreseeable future.

Market Concentration

No systematic studies have been identified that examine concentration in the book industry, although Bagdikian (1992) admonishes the increasing conglomeration in the book industry. To determine concentration in the book industry, the author calculated the top four (CR4) and top eight (CR8) concentration ratios using 1993 data from several different sources.

The CR4 ratio measured 30 percent, whereas the CR8 ratio was calculated at 50 percent. These calculations are well below levels that indicate a concentrated market. However, the fact that in 1993 the top eight (publicly reporting) firms accounted for 50 percent of the revenues in the book industry out of more than seven hundred publishers indicates a two-tiered market structure, with one set of large firms collecting half of the revenues and a large number of smaller companies sharing the remaining half.

Regulatory Forces Impacting the Book Industry

Like the magazine industry, the book industry does not encounter any direct governmental regulation beyond that imposed on other types of business activity. Perhaps the most important regulatory actions in the book industry over the past two decades have concerned copyright laws.

U.S. copyright law was revised during the 1970s, with several key changes impacting international markets. During the 1990s, publishers have taken advantage of international copyright protection of their works. Exports of book shipments account for nearly 10 percent of industry revenues, whereas foreign payments to domestic publishers have risen steadily during the 1990s. It is estimated that international royalty rights and translations could reach one billion dollars by the end of the decade (*U.S. Industrial Outlook*, 1994).

Environmental concerns over the use of recycled paper will remain an important regulatory issue in the coming years. Libraries are creating more demands on publishers to provide books that use recycled, as well as acid-free, paper—both of which raise the costs of publishing. It is unclear if self-regulatory efforts will be enough to thwart possible governmental intervention.

Technological Forces Impacting Books

As in other media industries, technology is affecting the book industry. Perhaps the greatest change has been the expansion of books into nonprint formats, beginning with audio versions of popular works. Audio books have proven to be very successful since their introduction during the early 1980s. Audio books complement hard and softcover editions, and tend to reach readers who have less time for reading.

CD-ROM technology represents many exciting opportunities for the book industry. The CD-ROM format allows for a visually pleasing design by incorporating sound and full-motion video to enhance textual presentation. Reference books such as encyclopedias and other works produced on CD-ROM are being met with approval by consumers. Demand for CD products is likely to be slow at the consumer level until more computer households become equipped to use the technology.

At the same time, the educational market is quickly adapting to CD technology. Some textbook publishers are beginning to offer CD supplements as a complement to traditional texts. For example, Wadsworth Publishing has developed an interactive CD to be used in conjunction with a television production course in which users learn various aspects of production. Allyn & Bacon is offering a CD version of different news clips from the Cable News Network to supplement a popular textbook used in an introductory mass media course.

Schools, institutions and libraries are also fueling interest in CD-ROM products. As schools upgrade, more CD-ROM access will become available. Many libraries are developing electronic reference systems, while increasing funding for CD applications. This in turn will spur publishers to develop even more products using the CD format. The potential applications of CD-ROM technology in the book publishing industry appears unlimited.

Book publishers are also taking advantage of the Internet to open new revenue streams. As this book was being prepared for publication, several publishers had developed "home pages" for computer users to access via the World Wide Web. For example, Simon & Schuster's "Information Superlibrary" connects users to more than twelve hundred online computer books, including several with clickable covers, tables of contents and sample chapters (*Edupage,* 1995). Publishers allow computer users to browse electronically through their holdings, and can even make purchases online at a direct discount. All major publishers will soon be accessible via the Internet.

Finally, other publishers are taking a new look at television as a way to market books. Most programs on books have traditionally been found only on the Public Broadcasting Service (PBS). But with several major book publishers heavily involved in the electronic media, more programs are in development to create interest in books, some designed for broadcast television and others targeted toward cable audiences (Cox, 1993).

The Economic Future of the Book Industry

Overall, the book industry is projected to perform favorably over the next several years, averaging around a 7 percent growth rate through 1997 (Veronis, Suhler and Associates, 1994). By 1997, consumer book revenues are expected to reach $19.2 billion, followed by professional books at $4.9 billion and educational books at $2.5 billion for a total of $29.6 billion (Veronis, Suhler and Associates, 1994).

The annual output of 50,000 titles per year is likely to increase as a result of expanded retailing efforts and an improving national economy. Some increase in book mergers and acquisitions may emerge as publishers seek partners in developing products for nonprint markets (*U.S. Industrial Outlook,* 1994).

Expanding markets through the development of nonprint formats will create new revenue streams for publishers over the next several years. As mentioned in the previous section, audio books, CD-ROM and the Internet represent alternative markets to traditional publishing.

International publishing should become a stronger presence in the next few years, thanks in part to the passage of the North American Free Trade Agreement (NAFTA), which will encourage greater commerce between the United States, Canada and Mexico. Further, international copyright protection for U.S. publishers has been enhanced through the General Agreement on Tariffs and Trade (GATT), particularly in regions where copyright provisions have been less than ideal, such as Asia, the Middle East and Eastern Europe (*U.S. Industrial Outlook,* 1994). These actions should produce expanded exports and royalty payments to book publishers.

Summary

Book publishing has existed since the 15th century as a form of mass media, and it remains a viable industry today. Book publishers draw revenues through the sale of books in three major markets: consumer, professional and educational. Demand for books is influenced by several microeconomic and macroeconomic factors.

The consumer market is the largest market, accounting for nearly 75 percent of all publishing revenues. The consumer market consists of adult and juvenile fiction, paperbacks and other subcategories primarily sold through retail outlets and bookstores. Professional books include medical, legal and business publications. Educational books are divided into two submarkets, the elementary and high school, or elhi, market, and the college textbook market.

There are hundreds of book publishers, although several large media companies capture most of the book industry revenues. Among the major domestic and international publishers are Time Warner, Viacom, Bertelsmann, News Corporation and International Thompson. The book industry operates under a monopolistic competitive market structure.

Recent regulatory actions in the book industry have resulted in expansion of copyright to the international arena, resulting in higher revenues for royalties and translation rights. Libraries continue to ask publishers to produce materials using recycled paper and acid-free paper to ease environmental concerns. Both recycled paper and acid-free paper raise the costs of book publishing.

Publishers are aggressively marketing books in nonprint formats. Audio books, introduced during the 1980s remain a popular format. Reference works are now available on CD-ROM, with other products in progress. Many publishers have found the Internet to be a source of new customers.

The book industry is expected to grow at a rate of 7 percent through 1997, when total revenues are expected to reach nearly $30 billion.

Discussion Questions

1. How has the book industry changed during its history? How is technology impacting the book industry?
2. Identify and discuss the different publishing markets within the book industry.
3. Describe the book industry in terms of market structure.
4. How has book retailing changed over the years? What is a book superstore, and how does it differ from the typical bookstore?

Exercises

1. Compare bestseller lists found in several different sources such as *The New York Times* Sunday edition, the *Chronicle of Higher Education* and your local newspaper. Are the lists similar or different? Why?
2. Visit a local bookstore in a shopping mall or retail outlet. Find out how many titles are in stock. If possible, visit a book superstore if one is available in your area for comparison.
3. Find out what audio books are the most popular in your community. What types of audiences use audio books?
4. If possible, try to find a reference work available on CD-ROM, such as *Grolier's Encyclopedia* or the *Encyclopedia Britannica.* What does this format offer compared to the standard encyclopedia?
5. If you have Internet access, locate a the major book publisher on the net and examine the material you discover online. Write a brief report on your findings.

References

Bagdikian, B. H. (1992). *The Media Monopoly*, 4th ed. Boston: Beacon Press.

Cox, M. (1993). TV stations see literary future: Shows on books. *The Wall Street Journal*, July 7, pp. B1, B7.

Cox, M. and Roberts, J. L. (1994). Mergers & manners. *The Wall Street Journal,* July 6, pp. A1, A12.

Edupage (1995, February 12). Superlibrary web sites.

Greco, A. N. (1993). Publishing economics: Mergers and acquisitions in the U.S. Publishing Industry: 1980–1989. In: Alexander, A., Owers, J., and Carveth, R. (eds.). *Media Economics: Theory and Practice*. New York: Lawrence Erlbaum Associates, pp. 205–224.

Standard & Poor's (1994). *Standard & Poor's Industry Surveys*. New York: Standard & Poor's.

U.S. Industrial Outlook (1994). Washington, DC: U.S. Department of Commerce.

Veronis, Suhler and Associates (1994). *Communications Industry Report*. New York: Veronis, Suhler and Associates.

Vivian, J. (1995). *The Media of Mass Communication,* 3rd ed. Needham Heights, MA: Allyn & Bacon.

5

The
Future
of
Media
Economics
Research

14

THE FUTURE OF MEDIA
ECONOMICS RESEARCH

In this summary chapter you will:

- Review how consolidation and conglomeration, technology, global-ization and regulatory trends are changing media markets and industries.

- Consider questions about the future of media economics research, and areas for further study.

W hat does the future hold for the study of media economics? How will media economics research evolve in the coming years? This summary chapter examines these questions by centering on some of the trends and patterns observed in the preceding chapters on individual media industries. The goal of this chapter is not to offer specific predictions, but rather to offer some educated assumptions about how the study of media economics will evolve based on current developments in the field.

The industry chapters in this text illustrate the diverse range of economic activities taking place across the mass media. At the same time, several trends run across many media industries. Among the most important similarities are the increasing levels of conglomeration and consolidation, changes in technology, the impact of globalization and regulatory forces. Here, we take a closer examination at each of these trends.

Trends Across Media Industries

Conglomeration/Consolidation. Increasing levels of industry consolidation were found across several media industries examined in this text. Over the years, mergers and acquisitions have reduced the number of players in many media industries to a handful of powerful conglomerates. Ozanich and Wirth (1993) identify four factors driving media mergers and acquisitions: (a) the growth of the media; (b) significant barriers to entry in many media markets, raising interest in existing firms with established market share and cash flow; (c) relaxation of regulatory hurdles that have prevented mergers; and (d) tax advantages for buyers. Several media industries such as newspapers, cable television, motion pictures and the recording industry were found to be heavily concentrated.

For example, companies such as Time Warner, Viacom, Sony and News Corporation produce and distribute products across a range of different markets (see Table 14-1). Horizontal expansion is one way companies are maximizing economic potential, and vertical integration is another method found among several media companies. By increasing their size and market share within an industry, companies are able to lower economies of scale, develop different revenue streams for the same product, and maximize shareholder value (Turow, 1992).

At the same time, industry concentration raises issues and concerns regarding the presentation of diverse views, particularly in the dissemination of news and informational products (Bagdikian, 1992). For the most part, regulators, especially in the United States, have shown less concern with media concentration and consolidation than with other more pressing domestic issues. We can expect further consolidation in some industries, particularly radio and television, in the years ahead.

Will all of this consolidation eventually result in a world dominated by a powerful oligopoly of media conglomerates? Trends suggest that this is possible, although it will likely be well into the next century before such a scenario unfolds. Media economics researchers should continue to observe and analyze the impact and effect of industry consolidation on both the market level and the consumer level, and provide recommendations for policy and regulatory action.

Technology. Another driving force across the media industries is in the area of technology. Innovations in the development of both hardware and software applications are creating new markets for media-related products. Companies, as well as consumers, are struggling to keep up with the numerous changes brought about by technological growth and development.

In the electronic media industries, the growth of digital technology is changing ways to distribute programming and increasing the number of available channels to consumers. Interactive applications for television, which in 1993 totaled an estimated $12 billion, mostly from the sale of video games, is expected to mushroom to nearly $22 billion by 1998 according to Veronis,

Table 14-1. Examples of media conglomerates across industries (industry in which firm is involved)

Firm	Radio	TV	Cable	PC/PPV	Film	Records	Newspapers	Magazines	Books
Time Warner		X	X	X	X	X		X	X
Sony					X	X			
Viacom		X	X	X	X	X			
News Corp (Fox)		X	X		X		X	X	X
Bertelsmann						X		X	X

Note: PC/PPV, premium cable/pay-per-view.

Suhler and Associates (Veronis, Suhler and Associates, 1994).

The print industries, as well as other media industries, are using the Internet to help market information on various products and services to consumers. Hundreds of media companies have home pages featuring text, video and audio information available through the World Wide Web.

Will consumers adopt many of the new technological services to be offered by media companies? How many of these new innovations will survive? More importantly, how much will consumers be willing to spend on these new products and services? Media economics research will help identify the demand for interactive and digital services, as well as new hardware and software products across the media industries.

Globalization. Globalization is another trend across many media industries reviewed in this text (Carveth, 1992). Economic growth and expansion are underway in many areas of the world, strengthened by the unification of the European Economic Community, economic development of countries in the Pacific Rim, and the North American Free Trade Agreement (NAFTA). These factors have opened up new markets for trade and commerce, especially in regards to media products and services.

Most domestic markets in the United States are already very saturated. For example, 99 percent of all households have a radio and television receiver, 95 percent of all households have a telephone, 79 percent have a VCR and 62 percent subscribe to cable (Veronis, Suhler and Associates, 1994). The situation is much different in the international marketplace. Europe and other areas offer excellent opportunities for business expansion and development [see, for example, Brauchili and Witcher (1993); Carveth, Owers and Alexander (1993); Jensen (1993) and (1994); Roberts (1994); Shirozu (1995); and Valente (1994)].

The United States has been a major exporter of media content products, but its future as a world leader has declined as a result of the rise of powerful media companies from other countries such as Bertelsmann, Sony, News Corporation (Carveth, Owers and Alexander, 1993). Hirsch (1992) explains that the globalization of media content, production and technology raises significant questions for further study, including issues related to media ownership, control and audience effects. Media economics can help provide answers to these important questions.

Regulatory forces. The Telecommunications Act of 1996, discussed at different points throughout the text, will lead to significant changes among many U.S. media industries, especially those making up the electronic media. The exact impact of this sweeping legislation will take time to sort out. In theory, the new reforms should spur competition, particularly among the broadcast, cable, and telephone industries. In practice, competition may not occur as fast as regulators would prefer, nor achieve the social goals of creating an affordable and accessible electronic superhighway envisioned in the legislation.

In the short run, conglomeration will escalate with the relaxation on the number of broadcast stations an individual company may own. More concentration will take place in many industries. In fact, it appears several major corporations such as Disney, Time Warner, News Corporation, Bertelsmann, and perhaps Sony will dominate the global media marketplace well into the 21st century.

Policy decisions, both at the domestic and global levels, need to be carefully studied to determine their effectiveness as well as their shortcomings. Media economics researchers will continue to play an important role in analyzing the regulatory actions and their impact on consumers.

The judicial system has also played a significant role in reshaping the electronic media landscape in the United States. The courts first opened the door for telephone companies to compete directly with cable television for subscribers, and they also have allowed cable operators to enter the telephone market (Pearl, 1993).

Questions for Further Study

The trends reviewed in the previous section of the chapter indicate media economics research will not only be an important field for future study, but that changes may be necessary in how to approach future research. For example, consolidation, technology, globalization and regulation are resulting in changes in media product markets. Markets are no longer separated by distinct lines of demarcation. It is becoming more and more difficult for media economic researchers to address the critical question of "what is the market?" The blurring of markets, along with the multiple revenue streams or windows for media content products, make differentiating the market a significant challenge for media economics research.

Coupled with the changes in studying individual markets are the likely changes in understanding and analyzing market structure. Will monopoly, oligopoly and monopolistic competition continue to be the best ways to classify and describe the structure of media markets? Or will new combinations and configurations be necessary?

For example, consider the newspaper industry, which primarily operates in a monopolistic environment. Do we continue to consider the newspaper a monopoly when it develops interactive and multimedia products for consumers in conjunction with the daily newspaper? Hardly. But how do we address these changes? Further, how will changes in market structure impact market conduct and performance? These questions raise issues regarding how we theorize market structures, as well as how we can evaluate and measure media markets in the future.

Finally, how do we study the impact of all of these changes in economic structure on the individual firms involved in these evolving markets? And what sort of impact will these changes have on society, both domestically and from an international perspective? Which approaches and methodologies will provide us with the data we need to answer these questions effectively? The impact on individual firms and society at large is another issue that must be considered in determining a course for further study.

Obviously, more questions than answers are raised by a discussion of how media economics research will change as a result of major trends impacting the media industries. Media economics research has many exciting challenges ahead as it attempts to sort out and analyze the complex and changing world in which the mass media industries operate.

Summary

The mass media industries are changing and adapting due to the influence of several major trends occurring across markets and industries. Industry consolidation is one of the most significant trends, fueled by an increase in mergers and acquisitions across the media industries. The result has been increasing concentration of control in many media industries, particularly in newspapers, cable television, motion pictures and the recording industry.

Technology is another trend shaping media markets. Innovations in new hardware and software products and services are creating new markets for media firms. Interactive and multimedia applications, along with products developed for the Internet, are growing rapidly.

Globalization of media products and services is the result of a saturated domestic U.S. market and strong opportunities for economic growth in other areas of the world, especially in Europe and the Pacific Rim. The NAFTA will encourage more U.S. trade and development with Canada and Mexico. The United States continues to play an important role in serving as the major exporter of media products, but its overall position as the world leader has declined in recent years.

Regulatory reforms, such as the Telecommunications Act of 1996, will lead to major structural changes across several media industries. The law, intended to foster competition primarily among the broadcast, cable and telephone industries, is the most sweeping legislation passed by Congress since the original Communications Act of 1934.

These trends raise significant challenges to the future study of media economics. The blurring of market boundaries and changes in market structure, conduct and performance raise questions about traditional methods used to evaluate media markets, media firms and societal impact. Media economics research will be challenged to address these and other issues in the years ahead.

Discussion Questions

1. What are some of the reasons given for so many mergers and acquisitions across the media industries?
2. How is technology changing the makeup and structure of media markets?
3. Globalization is a growing trend across the media industries. Why is there so much interest in the international marketplace for media product and services?
4. How will the changing structure of media markets impact the study of media economics? How will this impact future research?

Exercises

1. Conduct an ownership study of the local media in the market in which you currently reside. Who owns the local newspaper, broadcast stations, cable systems, etc.? What other media properties do they own?
2. Select a domestic-based company involved in some area of the mass media, and conduct research to determine the degree of international ventures and expansion. Prepare a report on your findings.
3. If you have Internet access, compare and contrast home pages of different media companies and services. Report on the types of things you find at the home pages.
4. Think about how industry structure may change in the future from the traditional models of monopoly, oligopoly and monopolistic competition. What other types of market structures are possible?
5. What do you envision as the major challenges facing media economics research in the future? What suggestions do you have for improving media economics research?

References

Bagdikian, B. (1993). *The Media Monopoly*, 4th ed. Boston: Beacon Press.

Brauchili, M. W. and Witcher, S. K. (1993). News Corp. purchases majority stake in Star TV of Asia for $525 million. *The Wall Street Journal*, July 27, p. B8.

Carveth, R. (1992). The reconstruction of the global media marketplace. *Communication Research* 19(6):705–723.

Carveth, R., Owers, J., and Alexander, A. (1993). The global integration of the media industries. In: Alexander, A., Owers, J., and Carveth, R. (eds.). *Media Economics: Theory and Practice*. New York: Lawrence Erlbaum Associates, pp. 331–354.

Hirsch, P. M. (1992). Globalization of mass media ownership. *Communication Research* 19(6):677–681.

Jensen, E. (1993). NBC purchases majority stake in global channel. *The Wall Street Journal*, October 4, p. B5.

Jensen, E. (1994). NBC creates broad alliance with TV Azteca. *The Wall Street Journal*, May 16, pp. A3, A6.

Ozanich, G. W. and Wirth, M. O. (1993). Media mergers and acquisitions: An overview. In: Alexander, A., Owers, J., and Carveth, R. (eds.). *Media Economics: Theory and Practice*. New York: Lawrence Erlbaum Associates, pp. 115–133.

Pearl, D. (1993). Cox envisions global pipeline for TV and phone signals. *The Wall Street Journal*, March 3, p. B4.

Roberts, J. L. (1994). News Corp.'s Murdoch outlines plans for TV programming on global basis. *The Wall Street Journal*, February 14, p. B8.

Shirozu, N. (1995). After years of static, Japanese cable changes channels. *The Wall Street Journal*, February 9, p. B4.

Turow, J. (1992). The organizational underpinnings of contemporary media conglomerates. *Communication Research* 19(6):682–704.

Valente, J. (1994). Global TV-news race heats up—but is payoff there? *The Wall Street Journal*, August 19, pp. B1–B2.

Veronis, Suhler and Associates (1994). *Communications Industry Report*. New York: Veronis, Suhler and Associates.

Supplements

REFERENCE SOURCES FOR MEDIA ECONOMICS RESEARCH

Many of the following sources will be available at university and public libraries. Call numbers are provided where possible.

Reference Sources on Corporations

NATIONAL DIRECTORIES

Directories may list corporate addresses, officers, annual sales, number of employees, and SIC* codes. Look at the preface of each volume to determine the extent and type of coverage.

HC102.2 .B2 Dun & Bradstreet, Inc. *America's Corporate Families: Billion Dollar Directory.* (Continues *Billion Dollar Directory*). Same format as *Million Dollar Directory* (see below).

HG4057 .A145 Dun & Bradstreet, Inc. *America's Corporate Families and International Affiliates.* 1983 to present. The international companion to *America's Corporate Families.* Same format as *Million Dollar Directory* (see below).

HG4057 .A219 *Directory of Corporate Affiliations.* (continues *Who Owns Whom*) 2 v. 1973 to present. Brief profile of parent companies, cross-reference index to subsidiaries, geographic, SIC*, and "Who's Where" index, for public and some private companies.

HG4057 .A22 *Dun's Business Rankings.* 1982 to present. Public and private businesses ranked within industry category and state, by size, sales, employees; includes stock ticker symbol cross reference.

---

*Standard Industrial Classification: A list of SIC code numbers is on the introductory pages of the Dun's publications and of *F & S Index.* For more detail, see *Standard Industrial Classification Manual* (HF1041.U613 Ref.).

HC102
.D8

Dun & Bradstreet, Inc. *Million Dollar Directory.* 5 v. 1959 to present. Includes roster of parent companies, parent/subsidiary cross references, brief profile of public and private companies (alphabetically), geographic and SIC* code indexes.

HG4057
.A4

Standard & Poor's Corporation. *Standard & Poor's Register of Corporations, Directors and Executives.* For public companies, corporate listings (v. 1), directors and executives (v. 2), and index (v. 3). 1973–present.

HG4057
.A56

Ward's Business Directory of U.S. Private and Public Companies. Annual. 4 v.

COMPANY OVERVIEWS

HG4057
.A28617

Hoover's Handbook of American Business. Reference Press, Inc.: Austin, TX. Profiles of 500 American-based companies. Divided into four sections: (1) A review of basic business concepts; (2) Lists of the largest companies overall and largest companies in various industries; (3) 500 company profiles arranged alphabetically; (4) Indexes by industry and location.

HG4057
.A286

Hoover's Masterlist of Major U.S. Companies. Contains information on 4,812 publicly listed U.S. companies, the top 500 largest private companies, 500 fastest growing companies and the 200 most important foreign companies. Entries include address, phone and fax numbers, Chief Executive Officer and Chief Financial Officer names, number of employees, stock symbol and exchange (if public), ownership (if private), and industry name.

HG4905
.M815

Moody's Handbook of Common Stocks. New York: Moody's Investors Service. Provides basic financial and business information on over 900 stocks with high investor interest. Information is arranged in one-page format, with chart showing stock performance since 1979 (where applicable). Revised quarterly.

HG4501
.S7664

Standard & Poor's Corporation. *Standard Corporation Records.* No cumulations; regularly updated. Includes company history, financial information, subsidiaries.

JOURNAL INDEXES

Business Periodicals Index. New York: Wilson. 1958–present. Indexes more than 275 periodical titles.

Predicasts F & S United States. 1960 to present. Two sections. Section 1 by SIC number; section 2 alphabetically by name of company.

The *Wall Street Journal Index.* 1957 to present. First half of volume indexes by name of company; second half indexes general news. Back issues of the *Wall Street Journal* are likely to be on microfilm.

Reference Sources on Industries

GENERAL REFERENCE SOURCES

HC106.6   *Standard & Poor's Industry Surveys.* New York: Standard and
.S74   Poor's Corporation. 1973 to present. Industry analyses and comparative financial statistics for major companies in each featured industry. Published quarterly.

U.S. Industrial Outlook. Washington, DC: U.S. Government Printing Office. Published 1960 to 1994. Information on recent trends and outlook for over 200 industries.

The Value Line Investment Survey. New York: A. Bernhard, n.d. Reports on 76 industry groups and analyzes approximately 1,500 stocks.

STATISTICAL SOURCES

American Statistics Index. Washington, DC: Congressional Information Service. 1973 to present. *A Comprehensive Guide and Index to the Statistical Publications of the U.S. Government.* Provides citations to statistical sources.

HF5003   *Irwin Business and Investment Almanac.* Homewood, IL: Busi-
.D68a   ness One Irwin. 1994. (Continues *Business One Irwin Business*
1994   *and Investment Almanac* 1991–1993 and *Dow Jones Business and Investment Almanac* 1982 to 1990.) Includes 1- to 3-page tables on trends and forecasts on 21 major industry groups; also stock market averages (charts) by industry group along with many other statistical tables and charts.

Predicasts Basebook. Cleveland, OH: Predicasts, Inc. 1974 to present. Compiles forecasts on products, markets, industry and economic aggregates for United States and North America as reported in trade and business press. Arranged by SIC numbers.

Predicasts Forecasts. Cleveland, OH: Predicasts, Inc. 1974 to present. Short- and long-range forecast statistics. Current journal citations accompany all data.

qZ7551
.K46
1985
Sourcebook of Global Statistics. New York: Facts on File. 1985. Reviews and provides tables of contents and bibliographic data for 209 statistical publications. Subject index.

Statistical Reference Index. Washington, DC: Congressional Information Service. 1980 to present. Selective guide to American statistical publications from sources other than the U.S. government.

INDUSTRY FINANCIAL/OPERATING RATIOS

Industry Norms and Key Business Ratios. New York: Dun & Bradstreet Credit Services. 1982 to present. Formerly *Dun & Bradstreet's Key Business Ratios* (1979 to 1981).

RMA Annual Statement Studies. Philadelphia: Robert Morris Associates. 1977 to present. (Previous title: Robert Morris Associates. *Annual Statement Studies.*

INDEXES TO JOURNAL ARTICLES

HF5681
.R25T68
Troy, Leo. *Almanac of Business and Industrial Financial Ratios.* Englewood Cliffs, NJ: Prentice-Hall. 1971 to present.

Business Periodicals Index. New York: H. W. Wilson, Co. 1958 to present. Indexes more than 275 business periodical titles.

Predicasts F & S Index: United States. Cleveland, OH: Predicasts, Inc. Indexes 750 financial and business publications which contain company, product and industry information.

Public Affairs Information Service (PAIS). New York: *Bulletin.* 1915 to present. A selective subject listing in the areas of economic and social conditions, public administration and international relations. Includes books, government documents and journals.

ADDITIONAL INDUSTRY SOURCES

HF5351
.E52
Encyclopedia of Business Information Sources, 8th ed. 1991/92. Detroit, MI: Gale Research, Inc., Comprehensive bibliography of

specialized publications on many industries.

HF5351
.D3
1993
Business Information Sources, Rev. ed. Berkeley, CA: University of California Press. 1993. Selected, annotated list of business books and reference sources, including online databases and CD-ROMs.

General Media Sources

YEARBOOKS AND DIRECTORIES

HE8689
.B771
Broadcasting/Cablecasting Yearbook (title varies, 1935 to present). Current industry information. Includes programming information, some federal rules; describes major markets; lists producers, distributors and production services; directory of radio, television and cable stations.

PN1990
4.D5
1989
Broadcast Communications Dictionary, 3rd ed., rev., 1989. New York: Greenwood Press.

PN4709
.E44
Editor and Publisher International Yearbook. 1920/21– . List of U.S. dailies and weeklies and Canadian and foreign weeklies with management and production information including circulation, rates, editors, etc.

Z6951
.A97
Gale Directory of Publications and Broadcast Media. Detroit, MI: Gale Research Inc. 1990 to present.

TK6540
.T453
Television and Cable Factbook. Washington, DC: Television Digest. 1944 to present.

Z6951
.W6
Working Press of the Nation. Annual. Chicago: National Research Bureau, Inc. Directory covering newspapers, magazines, radio and television, feature writers photographers and internal publications.

INDEXES AND ABSTRACTS

P87
.C59733
Communication Abstracts. Beverly Hills, CA: Sage. 1978 to present.

Dissertation Abstracts International. Ann Arbor, MI: University

Microfilms. 1938 to present. May be available in hardcover, microfilm, or CD-ROM formats. Check your local library.

Humanities Index. New York: H. W. Wilson. 1974 to present.

Index to the Times. Reading, England: Research Publications. 1906 to present.

PN4725
.D67

Journalism Abstracts. Columbia, SC: Association for Education in Journalism and Mass Communication. 1963 to present.

P87
.M318
1987

Index to Journals in Communication Studies through 1985. Annandale, VA: Speech Communication Association. 1987.

New York Times Index. New York: New York Times. 1913 to present.

PAIS Bulletin. New York: Public Affairs Information Service. 1915 to present.

Wall Street Journal Index. New York: Dow Jones. 1957 to present.

AI3
.T44

Television News Index and Abstracts: A Guide to the Videotape Collection of the Network Evening News Programs. Nashville, TN: Vanderbilt Television News Archives. 1968 to present. Also available online through gopher.

Electronic Reference Resources

ABI INFORM: Updated monthly, this database covers five years for about 800 business and management periodicals worldwide; 300 core titles are covered fully. Subject areas include accounting, banking, data processing (DP), economics, finance, human resources, insurance, general management, law and tax, organizational behavior and administration (OBA) and management science, marketing, advertising, sales, real estate, public administration, new product development and telecommunications. There are full citations and abstracts of about 200 words.

BUSINESS DATELINE: This product, updated monthly, provides access to hard-to-find, regional business information. It covers most of the same materials as ABI INFORM from 200 local, state and regional business publications. These articles are the full text of the publication. Press releases from Business Wire provide a corporate perspective on events and people.

COMPACT DISCLOSURE: This product consists of business and financial information extracted from 10K reports that public companies file with the Securities and Exchange Commission. It includes all financial statements (three to seven years for comparison purposes), subsidiaries, description of the business, officers and directors, stock information, president's letter and management discussion for over 11,000 public companies. Financial data can be converted to files that can be imported as numbers directly into spreadsheets.

WALL STREET JOURNAL: This is a full text product containing every article including daily stock market reports, finance, investment, and business oriented news. Its coverage runs from 1989 and is updated monthly.

INFOTRAC BUSINESS INDEX: This product contains bibliographic references to and abstracts of articles from more than 800 business, management and trade publications, including *The Wall Street Journal*, *The New York Times*, *Asian Wall Street Journal*, and *Financial Times of Canada*. This database contains back files to 1982 and is updated monthly.

DUN'S MILLION DOLLAR DIRECTORY: This database provides comprehensive business information on 161,000 U.S. public and private companies. Listings are limited to companies with $25 million or more in sales, or 250+ employees, or a net worth of $500,000 or more. File records can be searched by geographical area, primary and secondary SIC codes, annual sales, or number of employees. This is a useful tool for job searching.

MORNING STAR MUTUAL FUNDS ONDISC: This product provides such items as description and analysis, basic operating facts, and several years of statistics for total return, income, capital gains, and performance/risk factors.

FIRST SEARCH is an online service that offers access to a number of databases useful to business researchers: Articles1st, Contents1st, ERIC, the GPO Monthly Catalog, and WorldCat, an electronic card catalog of 24 million bibliographic records representing the holdings of 13,000 libraries worldwide. Check to see if this service is available at your library.

COMMONLY USED FINANCIAL RATIOS

Financial ratios are useful in determining the financial viability of a corporation. Most ratios can be calculated using the financial statements found in a corporate annual report. Several research sources list a number of financial ratios for both individual companies and industries. The following are some of the most common ratios used in financial and performance analysis.

Liquidity Ratios

CURRENT RATIO

$$\frac{\text{Current Assets}}{\text{Current Liabilities}}$$

ACID TEST RATIO

$$\frac{\text{Liquid Assets}}{\text{Current Liabilities}}$$

Debt Ratios

LEVERAGE RATIO

$$\frac{\text{Total Liabilities}}{\text{Total Assets}}$$

DEBT TO EQUITY RATIO

$$\frac{\text{Total Liabilities}}{\text{Total Equity}}$$

Capitalization Ratios

$$\frac{\text{Total Shares of Preferred Stock}}{\text{Total Shares of Common Stock}}$$

Long-term Liabilities
Total Shares of Common Stock

Common Growth Measures

GROWTH OF REVENUE
Current Period (month, quarter) Revenue–Previous Time Revenue
Previous Time Revenue

GROWTH OF OPERATING INCOME
Current Operating Income–Previous Operating Income
Previous Operating Income

GROWTH OF NET WORTH (Owner's Equity)
Current Period (month, quarter) Net Worth–Previous Time Net Worth
Previous Time Net Worth

GROWTH OF ASSETS
Current Period (month, quarter) Assets–Previous Time Assets
Previous Time Assets

Profitability Measures

RETURN ON SALES
Operating Income
Total Revenues

RETURN ON ASSETS
Operating Income
Total Assets

RETURN ON EQUITY
Operating Income
Owner's Equity

PRICE-EARNINGS (PE) RATIO
Market Price of a Share of Common Stock
Earnings Per Share

Profit Margins

CASH FLOW MARGIN

Cash Flow (After-tax net profit plus interest, depreciation, amortization)
Net Revenue (Revenues minus operating expenses)

NET PROFIT MARGIN

Net Profit (Revenues–expenses and taxes)
Total Revenues (Sales)

GLOSSARY OF KEY TERMS

addressable converter—a device used in the cable industry to decipher scrambled signals; necessary on most systems to receive pay-per-view programming.

allocative efficiency—occurs when an individual market functions at optimal capacity, spreading its benefits among both producers and consumers.

ATV—Advanced television system, which may be a forerunner of high definition television (HDTV).

barriers to entry—are normally thought of as obstacles new sellers must overcome before entering a particular market.

capitalization ratios—used to analyze the capital represented by both preferred and common stock.

churn—turnover of the cable television audience for both regular cable subscribers and premium channel subscribers. Cable operators are constantly marketing their services in different ways to potential new subscribers to minimize the effects of churn.

clustering—the merging of smaller cable systems into larger multiple system operators in specific regions. Clustering has become a common practice in the cable industry.

command economy—In this type of economy, the government makes all decisions regarding production and distribution. The government also establishes wages and prices and plans the rate of economic growth.

concentration—the number of producers or sellers in a given market.

concentration ratios—used to measure the degree of concentration in an industry; compares the ratio of total revenues of the major players to the revenues of the entire industry, using the top four firms (CR4) or the top eight firms (CR8).

consumption—the utilization of goods and resources to satisfy different wants and needs of consumers.

cost structures—the costs for production in a particular market.

cross-elasticity of demand—In the media industries, a number of competitors produce similar media content, and consumers often sample and substitute other media products regularly; this is known as cross-elasticity of demand.

DBS—direct broadcast satellites.

debt ratios—measure the debt of a firm or industry. Common debt measures include a leverage ratio and the debt-to-equity ratio.

demand—the measure of the quantity of a particular product or service that consumers will purchase at a given price.

demassification—describes how the magazine industry is targeting audiences with products designed to meet specific interests and needs.

digital technology—a distribution system that converts analog recordings into a binary code of 1s and 0s; excellent reproduction quality.

diversification—is the extent to which a company draws revenues across different markets or business segments.

dual product market—many media companies produce one product, but participate in two separate good and service markets aimed at audiences and advertisers.

duopoly—refers to radio ownership; duopoly rules were modified in 1992, allowing for multiple ownership of radio stations within the same geographical market.

economics—the study of how societies use scarce resources to produce valuable commodities and distribute them among different groups.

economies of scale—the decline in average cost that occurs as additional units of a product are created.

efficiency—the ability of a firm to maximize its wealth.

elasticity of demand—when a change in price results in a change in the quantity demanded by consumers. Demand can be elastic, inelastic or unit elastic.

equity—is concerned with the way in which wealth is distributed among producers and consumers in a market.

event television—another term for pay-per-view; audience members pick and choose among different content choices in the form of movies, sporting events, and specials.

exclusivity—term used in the premium cable industry; each service attempts to distinguish its service from that of other competitors with a unique package of feature films and other entertainment.

fiber optic cable—consists of several strands of a glass-like substance capable of transmitting modulated light via a laser, with a capacity nearly 600 times larger than coaxial cable.

franchise—term used in the cable industry to signify the awarding of a geographical area to a cable operator by a local government for the purpose of providing cable television service.

geographic regions—a way to define a market, along with the product dimensions.

growth measures—calculate the growth of revenue and assets over time, and also document historical trends.

HDTV—high definition television; touted as television of the future. HDTV employs digital technology and a higher resolution capacity.

Herfindahl-Hirschman Index (HHI)—The HHI is calculated by summing the squared market shares of all firms in a given market. A precise measure of industry concentration.

homes passed—in the cable industry, refers to homes that have access to cable television services. In 1995, homes passed by cable was around 94 percent of all television households in the United States.

industrial organizational model—a theoretical model that shows the relationships among market structure, conduct and performance.

industry—the number of sellers in a particular market.

insertion advertising—Insertion advertising occurs when national cable networks such as ESPN, MTV and USA offer advertising availabilities to local systems to "insert" local commercials.

interconnects—an interconnect exists where two or more operators join together to distribute advertising simultaneously over their respective systems.

invisible hand doctrine—theorized by Adam Smith, this doctrine suggests that the economy is directed by an unseen force to the benefit of all producers and consumers.

joint operating agreements (JOAs)—found in the newspaper industry. Under a JOA, editorial operations remain separate, but all other operations (printing, advertising, distribution, etc.) are combined.

liquidity ratios—include the quick ratio, the current ratio, and the acid test ratio. Measures ability to convert assets into cash.

local marketing agreement (LMA)—used in the broadcast industry; an LMA allows one station to take over marketing and programming of another station without releasing control of ownership.

Lorenz Curve—used in measuring industry concentration; it illustrates inequality of market share among different firms.

macroeconomics—examines the whole economic system, primarily studied at a national level. Macroeconomics includes topics such as economic growth indices, political economy and national production and consumption.

market—is where consumers and sellers interact with one another to determine the price and quantity of the goods produced. A market consists of a number of sellers that provide a similar product or service to the same group of buyers/consumers.

market conduct—the policies and behaviors exhibited by sellers and buyers in a market.

market performance—involves analyzing the ability of individual firms in a market to achieve goals based on different performance criteria.

market economy—a complex system of buyers, sellers, prices, profits and losses determines the answers to questions regarding production and distribution, with no government intervention.

microeconomics—centers on the activities of specific components of the economic system, such as individual markets, firms or consumers.

mixed economy—combinations of the market and command economies are referred to as a mixed economy.

media economics—is the study of how media industries use scarce resources to produce content that is distributed among consumers in a society to satisfy various wants and needs.

monopoly—a type of structure whereby a single seller of a product exists.

monopolistic competition—exists when there are many sellers offering products that are similar, but not perfect substitutes for one another.

multiple ownership rules—in the broadcast industry, refers to the limits imposed by the Federal Communications Commission on the number of stations in which an individual or group may hold ownership interests.

multiple system operators (MSOs)—term for large cable system operators such as Tele-Communications, Inc. and Time Warner.

multipoint multichannel distribution services (MMDS)—also referred to as wireless cable, offer programming packages via microwave transmission.

multiplexing—a technique that results in splitting programming among 2–3 channels; first introduced in the premium cable industry.

must carry—regulations that required cable operators to carry all local broadcast stations. Ruled unconstitutional in 1985.

near video-on-demand (NVOD) system—a type of television system of the future.

needs—basic items needed by individuals and society for survival.

network—in the broadcast industry, this term is used to describe a service that provides programming to affiliates.

oligopoly—a type of market structure that features more than one seller of a product. Products offered by the sellers may be either homogeneous or differentiated.

overbuilds—areas served by more than one cable system.

owned and operated stations—term used to describe network owned stations in the broadcast industry (referred to as O&O's).

PCS—personal communication services; new technology that will compete with cellular telephone service. PCS offer ways to exchange voice, data and other information.

perfect competition—a market structure characterized by many sellers in which the product is homogeneous and no single firm or group of firms dominates the market.

performance or profitability measures—used to measure the financial strength of a company or industry.

private companies—companies that are privately owned by individuals; cannot purchase stock or other ownership in private companies.

product differentiation—the subtle differences (either real or imagined) perceived by buyers to exist among products produced by sellers.

production—the actual creation of different goods for consumption.

progress—the ability of firms in a market to increase output over time.

PTAR—prime time access rule; prohibits affiliated stations in the top 50 TV markets from using off-network series during access time periods. Expires in August 1996.

public companies—publicly owned by individual and institutional stockholders who invest in a firm in hopes of obtaining profits through stock appreciation and corporate dividends.

resources—are defined in economic terms as items used to produce goods and services. Resources consists of both tangible and intangible items.

retransmission consent—outcome of the 1992 Cable Television Act, which allows broadcast stations to negotiate with cable operators for right to carry their signals.

satellite master antenna television (SMATV)—a form of private cable that is restricted to specific areas such as apartment and condominium complexes, motels and hotels.

scatter market—unsold advertising time that is retained by the network and offered during the television season.

supply—the amount of a product producers will offer at a certain price.

technical efficiency—involves using the firm's resources in the most effective way to maximize output.

tiers—cable industry term used to distinguish between different classes of service.

upfront market—network television advertising time purchased during the early summer months for the upcoming fall season.

utility—what consumers perceive in the way of satisfaction from a good or service.

value—the worth of a product or service; measured by an exchange in dollars or other monetary measure. Value changes over time.

vertical integration—occurs when a firm controls different aspects of production, distribution and exhibition of its products.

video compression—technology that allows compression of existing television signals to allow more expansion of channels. Employs digital technology to compress signals.

video dialtone (VDT) services—used to describe cable-like services, which will be offered by telephone companies.

wants—items individuals want to improve the quality of life, but are not really necessary for survival as are needs.

windows—describes multiple revenue streams, such as in the motion picture industry.

wireless cable—another term for MMDS services.

World Wide Web—a part of the Internet of computer networks; allows for the integration of text, voice and video data in the creation of various home pages of information that can be accessed by consumers.

INDEX

Please note that **bolded** pages refer to pages that contain tables or figures.